YOU CAN STILL
HIT THE MARK!
DISCOVER HOW PERSISTENCE
OVERCOMES
NATURAL TALENT

KEVIN *"HURRICANE"* **HUDSON**

authorHOUSE®

AuthorHouse™
1663 Liberty Drive
Bloomington, IN 47403
www.authorhouse.com
Phone: 1 (800) 839-8640

Published by AuthorHouse 10/10/2019

ISBN: 978-1-7283-3078-5 (sc)
ISBN: 978-1-7283-3077-8 (e)

Print information available on the last page.

Scripture quotations marked NIV are taken from the Holy Bible, New International Version®. NIV®. Copyright © 1973, 1978, 1984 by International Bible Society. Used by permission of Zondervan. All rights reserved. [Biblica]

This book is printed on acid-free paper.

Because of the dynamic nature of the Internet, any web addresses or links contained in this book may have changed since publication and may no longer be valid. The views expressed in this work are solely those of the author and do not necessarily reflect the views of the publisher, and the publisher hereby disclaims any responsibility for them.

CONTENTS

CHAPTER 1

PASSION FOUND

Holding my father's hand, feeling sort of scared yet excited in an odd way, we walked into a musty old tin building. Inside, a handful of people were standing in a loose rectangle. They moved on command, in unison, without looking at their leader, who was a large, balding fellow with a permanent grimace. His eyes were dark and seemed to stare deep inside each person as he walked through the crowd, analyzing each step and gesture. *"Ichi, ni, san!"* he shouted, as the participants completed certain moves.

Seeing a traditional karate class for the first time I was totally puzzled. A few weeks prior to this day I had witnessed a kid do karate in a talent show at my elementary school, but this was not what I had thought it would be like. The building was metal, with no air conditioning. The temperature had to be over ninety. The people doing the moves were barefoot, and dressed in identical uniforms. The kid in the talent show had worn a purple belt, but these people had gray belts. The flooring was multicolored, as though they hadn't had a large enough rug to cover the entire floor, and so they had each brought in a piece of carpeting. It was even put together with gray duct tape.

The leader looked up us with a disturbed look, as though we had unintentionally interrupted something important. The group didn't move. They all stood awkwardly, without acknowledging the leader had departed from his post to tend to us. My dad and I stood still not knowing whether to slide back out or stand our ground.

As the group stood silent and still, the leader walked over and greeted us with his stern look, "Hello, can I help you?" he said in a loud voice, evidently still accustomed to screaming at the group.

"We saw you were teaching karate here, and my son wants to try it," my dad answered

The large man smiled and the grimace on his face eased, but the creases remained prominent. "Well, I don't really teach children here. We primarily work with adults."

Just then the only lady in the group of statues, who were now shaking somewhat as they tried to maintain their positions, stood upright and walked over.

"My name is Angie," she said, "and this is Lamar. We'd be glad to let your son try training here with us." As I stared up at this small lady I could tell she was someone important to the large man, Lamar. His tone softened and his posture became less rigid, though he was still intimidating.

"Great! That sounds good," my dad exclaimed. "When can he come, and how much does it cost?"

Lamar returned to the class of frozen, shaking people, in a stealthy fashion so he would not be missed by us, as my dad stood discussing whether an eight year-old would be able to manage a class with a bunch of hardcore, militaristic karate nuts.

Angie began to speak, acknowledging that Lamar (or Sensei Nelson, as they called him) had drifted away. "He can come to any class we have. We have class Monday through Thursday from six to eight p.m. At his age, though, I don't know if he'll want to come that often."

"Well, we'll bring him when he needs to come if that's what he wants to do," my dad said.

"We just charge twenty-five dollars per month," Angie said.

My dad pulled out his worn wallet and gave Angie a twenty and a five. Then he looked down at me standing close beside and said, "Well, son, I guess we'll be here Monday at six." I was excited, but also a little nervous. There weren't any other little boys, the other participants seemed big and a little scary, but I agreed despite being a little apprehensive.

My dad yelled as Angie was turning away, and asked, "What does he need to wear?"

Angie turned. "He doesn't need a uniform or anything. Just let him wear his shorts and a t-shirt."

"Yes ma'am, will do," my dad replied, as he turned toward me and the metal door with the exit sign taped over the top.

During the weekend, I could hardly contain himself. I was excited, but still apprehensive. I had only seen one karate movie in my life, but after seeing the kid at my elementary school do karate in the talent competition I knew it was something I wanted to try.

Monday finally arrived, and it was a pretty normal day. I went to school as usual. It was spring, so flowers were in full bloom and grass was growing. It was getting hotter by the day as summer was fast approaching. Little did I know, I was about to embark on a life-changing event.

Very seldom are kids put into a position to discover their passion early. There are occasions when parents guide kids toward an activity, and the child may make a living out of that activity, but it is not truly a passion until one day they realize the parent or guardian knew better than they did what path to choose. For me, this was a paramount time in my life, directed by the providence of God.

On Monday after school I dashed home and got my homework done as fast as I could, then choked down a peanut butter and jelly sandwich. There was no uniform for me to put on so I grabbed a t-shirt and some shorts. As soon as I sat down on the couch, my mom shouted from the kitchen, "Your dad said to take you to karate about five-thirty, so make sure your homework is done."

"Yes ma'am," I answered.

The time finally arrived. I jumped into the car with mom and off we went to the dojo. Little did I know this would be the first of thousands of trips to the karate school or dojo, as they say in Japanese. Class started at six, so arriving at five-thirty gave me plenty of time to check out the place. My mom parked on the gravel lot, got out of the Buick, and walked me in through the open garage-style door. There were a few twenty-something men hanging around chatting inside, and that big man named Lamar. It wasn't long before I was told that Lamar was to be addressed as "Sensei," which translates to "one who has gone before" or "teacher."

Sensei didn't really have much interaction with me at this point. It was pretty much just do what everyone else does and stay out of the way, which is what I tried to do. I imitated every move to best of my ability. I went right along, just like I was meant to be there ... which many years later would prove to be the case.

During this first class, for some reason, Sensei chose to cover falling in addition to the normal curriculum for the day. Perhaps I should have gotten the hint, that maybe they didn't want me there, when all Sensei really wanted me to do that day was fall. I didn't care. I just knew I couldn't let that big man they all called Sensei be disappointed in my performance.

I followed along the entire two-hour session. I said nothing, but stayed intently focused on what was going on and what the gray-belted men were doing. Later on I came to realize the "gray" belts were actually black belts that had been worn so often they were starting to fade back to their original white color. Years later I was told by one of the senior students that if a student started at white belt and stayed until black, and did not give up, his belt would eventually fade back to the white color from which it started. Only then would the student be considered to really understand the art he was training in.

After the grueling first session one of the men in the class came over me with a big grin on his face.

"Hey, my name's Eddie. You did a super job your first day, hot shot!" he exclaimed as he patted me on the top of my head.

About that time my mom pulled into the gravel drive for pick up. I looked up at the sweaty, muscular man and said, "Thanks Eddie."

I jumped into mom's car and began the ride home. During the twelve-minute drive I told mom all about the cool stuff I had gotten to do in class. I was drenched with sweat, so mom in here motherly wisdom inquired, "Was it hard?"

"It was pretty hard mom, but I knew I couldn't quit."

One never knows which path to take as a young man or woman. The one thing that is known at the time the path is chosen is that it is the only one he or she can follow at that time. With the proper attitude and environment, even the most uninviting circumstances can be tolerable. Sometimes not knowing that one can stop and change directions is the greatest gift one could ever be given.

You never know what impact you have on people. My first class and introduction to martial arts training turned out to be the path God had placed before me.

SUREFIRE STRATEGY 1: Find your passion. Life moves quickly. The quicker you can find your passion and begin pursuing it, the better. Try things until you find that one thing that makes your heart race a little faster, that thing that wakes you up early to get started. Get good at that passion—so good that people will even pay you for doing it. Mark Twain said, "Make your vacation your vocation." You've got to work somewhere in life to make a living and provide for yourself, so why not do something you love?

SUREFIRE STRATEGY 2: Love your mom. No matter the type of relationship you've had with your mom, she gave birth to you. She went through the pain of carrying you and bringing you into this world in one piece, so give her respect.

SUREFIRE STRATEGY 3: Take action. There's a whole book in the Bible called Acts. Life is about action. You don't have to get things right; you just have to get things going. Education will come as you work through a project. If you wait until you've got it perfect to start, it'll never happen. That's like saying you'll have kids when you have enough money. All parents know that's not possible.

"'11 For I know the plans I have for you,' declares the LORD, 'plans to prosper you and not to harm you, plans to give you hope and a future.'" (Jeremiah 29:11)

CHAPTER 2

VALUABLE TRAINING

At fourteen, I was a tall drink of water. About five foot ten and 135 pounds, I was lean to say the least. Many people called me string bean and lanky—oh, how I hated the word "lanky"! But when those people saw me in a karate class and watched me do my thing, they no longer had an urge to poke fun, especially after seeing me spar.

I handled himself really well for an awkward teen. In fact, back in those days there would sometimes be some unruly characters who would pop into the school with challenges. Many times they had been drinking or were just a little too big for their britches.

Once a smaller man about 150 pounds' entered the school. The members of the dojo soon found out why. Everyone could tell he'd been drinking. He stood at the front with a smirk on his face after he walked in, just waiting for someone to approach. The instructor at the time wasn't one to take too kindly to this sort of arrogance. You have to be a little off to enter a martial arts school you've never been in and challenge someone to a fight. This man stood there, kind of wobbly in the wind. He finally shouted across the room, "I want to fight the baddest man here!"

The instructor walked over and spoke quietly to the fellow. As they spoke you could tell the newcomer was not welcoming the comments. He kept pointing to the taped ring on the floor, saying, "But I want to fight in that ring!" Finally, seeing how he was getting nowhere with this slightly inebriated man, the instructor pointed at me. I was usually at class way early, stretching and preparing. He told the man, "You can fight this kid, and if you beat him, then you can fight the toughest man in here."

The glassy-eyed fellow looked at the instructor, then back to me sitting on the floor in the split. He finally said, "I don't want to hurt no kid!" The instructor went on to assure him that he wouldn't hurt the kid, and besides, he had to fight the kid before he could fight the toughest you-know-what in the school. Reluctantly the newcomer followed the instructor across the floor to an old gym bag with some boxing gloves in it. The instructor pulled out a pair and gave them to the man, saying, "Put these on and I'll go get the kid for you."

The instructor walked quickly over to me sitting on the floor and explained I was going to get a little extra sparring in for the day. I loved to spar so I readily agreed and trotted over to my little gym bag with my sparring gear neatly inside. I pulled it all out quickly and put it on, piece by piece, then walked to the taped ring on the floor. The school guest was donning a set of Jhoon Rhee sparring gloves and no shoes.

I stood on the taped line and faced my opponent in the ring, the instructor began giving his final instructions. The instructor told the man to keep his hands up and protect himself at all times. Spectators started to gather around the square taped down on the floor, and the guest appeared to become more conscious of what he had gotten himself into. Before giving the command to fight, the instructor leaned over to me standing before this guy and gave his famous command: "Now I want you to bust him, okay?"

I just shook my head and held up my gloves in the ready position. We were given the command to bow to the referee and to each other. Even when you were fighting a drunk in the dojo you had to bow before starting. Karate always begins and ends with respect, even if one of the combatants is half intoxicated and fifteen years older than the other.

"Begin!" the instructor shouted.

We kind of danced around for a bit, just staring at one another.

The guest shouted to the instructor, "Man, I don't want to hurt this kid!"

"You'd better keep your hands up, 'cause he's gonna kick you," the instructor yelled back. After which he shouted to me, "Go ahead and kick him one time."

After hearing that, I didn't take my eyes off this opponent—I knew that was a no-no. I danced around until just the right opportunity arose and launched a right leg round kick, one of my favorite moves. The right leg easily swept over the protecting glove of the poor sitting duck and into his face. The man's head snapped back, hair flying. As his head came back up everyone noticed there was a little blood dripping from his nose. He was fully aware now that he was in a fight, embarrassed that a teenager had just about broken his nose in front of a bunch of strangers.

He snorted like a raging bull—not *the* Raging Bull, but the four-legged one. His breathing was shallow and loud. He lunged at me with a huge right-hand swing. In certain parts of the country this is call a "redneck swing." It missed me by a mile as I was pretty agile as young fighter, moving around effortlessly in the ring. The raging bull reset himself and decided that, since his first punch had missed, he'd launch the next one even harder.

When he turned his body to deliver what he intended to be a finishing blow, he had no idea that he was about to secure his own demise. I chambered my lead leg and extended it into the ribcage of this poor victim. A perfect side-thrust kick, striking the ribcage with the blade and heel of the foot. My foot appeared to sink into the man's abdominal region as it locked straight and as the man moved forward. Much like two cars hitting head-on, the force was now not just doubled but exponentially increased. The man slowly folded his entire body around my foot and leg. The crowd, which had been cheering, now stood in silence.

The man crumpled to the floor like a trampled aluminum can. Unable to breathe, he lay in a fetal position in the center of the ring. I withdrew my leg and set it back on the floor, I stood silent, peering at the man. Just then the instructor jumped in and said loudly and unnecessarily, "Break!" The crowd began to disperse back to their previous positions in the school area.

The instructor looked at me and said, "Turn around and kneel here."

I was not to face the falling combatant who was apparently injured on the floor. Even though the loud, disrespectful man had come into the school looking for trouble, the instructor treated him with respect and tried not to draw further attention to the fact that he had made a terrible mistake. I continued to remain kneeled down as instructed, while the teacher attempted to sit the wounded man up. The injured man sat up, but would not sit straight and hold his head up. He began to breathe, slowly and painfully. The instructor and the other onlookers knew that the guest was suffering from two things: a couple broken ribs and some terribly hurt pride. I had no idea I had broken the man's ribs.

Finally, gathering the man up, the instructor spoke to him empathetically: "That hurts, doesn't it?"

The guest, now perfectly sober, stood up, though he was bent over about forty-five degrees, grasped his side, said softly, "Yeah, it sure does."

"I guess you don't want to fight the toughest one here now? You couldn't even whoop our fourteen-year-old kid," the instructor said, rubbing salt into the man's wounds.

The instructor walked the injured man out and he departed quietly without causing any more ruckus. All this took place before class began, so the instructor shouted at me to take my gear off and get ready for class. I did so gladly, barely even sweating from this pre-class sparring match.

As the instructor shut the door behind the visitor, he turned to the class and yelled, "Line up!" which was the command to get on the floor in a straight line and kneel in position to begin class. The instructor walked by me, as I was seated at the end of the line. He patted me on the back and said, "Good job." Class began as usual, without any further acknowledgement of the incident. Even when I was picked up by my dad that night I didn't mention the episode.

I learned that night that there is a problem with thinking you're better than someone else, and sometimes you need to be taught a lesson by someone with a good side kick.

"Pride goes before destruction, a haughty spirit before a fall." (Proverbs 16:18)

We all have moments in life when we feel indestructible. We feel we can conquer the world with one arm and good chin. We must realize, though, that we ain't as special as we think. There is always someone who has come before who did it better. They may have not have been famous, they may have led a quiet life, but you can bet that, if they were a thinking person, they knew that humility often really hurts.

We have an infinite, omnipresent, omniscient God. How can a finite man even begin to judge His actions? There are people who question the existence of such a God. I ask them, "Would you say you know everything there is to know in the universe?" They always answer "No." Then my question to them is if they live only seventy or eighty years and do not know all there is in the universe, then how can they logically tell me there is no God. My friend, He's there! I'm sure you've been humbled by Him at some point, and I'm sure you've asked "Why?" I suggest to you, my friend, that "Why?" is not the question at that point when your life shatters in a thousand pieces. The questions is: "Who?"

SUREFIRE STRATEGY 4: Stay humble. No matter how tough you think you are, there is always someone out there who is tougher. To stay the best at something is knowing that we are one poor decision away from losing our reputation and our influence.

SUREFIRE STRATEGY 5: Learn to take a punch. There are times in your life when you will get hit. You may get hit physically, but I'm sure you'll get hit emotionally and spiritually as well. In life, you have to learn to roll with those punches. I recommend getting some training in martial arts, whether it is a boxing class, self-defense, karate, or Brazilian jujitsu. The world ain't getting safer and to protect yourself and your family you have to be trained. One of the worst things that could happen to you in a life-threatening altercation is to freeze. In that type of situation, ignorance kills.

SUREFIRE STRATEGY 6: Exercise and eat right. You only get one temple. You were created in God's image and I'm sure He wouldn't appreciate you throwing junk down the hatch every day of your life and sitting on the couch. If you stay sedentary too long you will rust. Your body was made to move and work. Join a gym and attend regularly, start a martial arts class, or join 9round.com (had to throw that in for my brother). Steady exercise can add years to your life and quality to your years. When it comes to diet, there are many options out there. If you just cut out sugars and fried foods you've won a large portion of the battle. When I competed, I found out very quickly that sugar would make you retain weight, and the older you get the more impact what you consume makes. Make sure to consult a dietician before going gung ho on something.

CHAPTER 3

MISSION CHOSEN

At this point as a teenager, I began to blossom as a martial artist and became well respected among those who passed through the school. I was now going on sixteen, and had chosen my path … or, rather, my path had been chosen for me. During my ascent through the belts I became aware of kickboxing, and after seeing it on television I aspired to try this new sport. Little did I realize that the man who is credited with bringing kickboxing to America would one day become my teacher and guide my training.

In the beginning I wasn't that athletically talented, but for some reason I had an amazing amount of natural determination. I would never quit. Sometimes this may have been out of ignorance; at other times it may have been because I didn't want to let anyone know I couldn't do something.

At fifteen I had my first kickboxing match. Early on as a karate student I had done several point tournaments. I did okay in these events, but had a problem controlling the power of my blows. Many tournaments would warn about and deduct points for excessive contact. Based on this, I figured kickboxing would be a good fit. I first did a three-rounder in a small town in North Carolina. This was the start of a career that would span decades, two world championships, hundreds of rounds of sparring, many stitches, broken bones, the loss of friends, and the gaining of some brothers, among many other things.

When first beginning this kickboxing quest, I desperately tried to find people who had connections in the new sport or who had competed in kickboxing at some level. There was a man on the edge of NC who had made a name for himself fighting at an elite level in the fetal stages of the sport. So I, with a fresh driver's license in my pocket, set out to drive the two-hour round trip each week for some extra sparring and kickboxing workouts. After doing some preliminary work, Ray, the veteran fighter, suggested that I could use a little boxing training.

When kickboxing first began evolving after its birth in America, most of the fighters were black belts who tried to use karate hand movements with kicks. These early fighters found out pretty quickly that a good jab is a hard thing to deal with in most bouts. Many bouts ended up with a journeyman boxer pitted against a karate guy with zero boxing experience. The journeyman boxer learned how to throw a simple front kick for the bout and went in full steam ahead. Once the boxer got inside the kicker's legs he'd receive a few good body shots from the experienced boxer and be done for the night, usually with cracked ribs and a sore ego.

The new training partner from the NC town had been a victim of a good boxer and told me as a hopeful future champ I needed to hone my boxing skills and learn some good boxing mechanics. There was a small boxing gym not far from the town in which some good boxers had trained.

On a hot Saturday morning in July I traveled the hour trip to a rundown barn-like structure in the foothills of the NC mountains. Upon arriving I parked my car and met Ray in the parking lot. We entered the barn through the side entrance, up a steep set of stairs. Ray pulled the door by the latch and it creaked back, releasing an aroma of sweat, tears, and heat, and the noise of a round timer, twirling jump ropes, and the *put-ab-u, put-ab-u, put-ab-u* of the speed bag.

An older fellow, with a whistle around his neck, named Jimmy, approached Ray with a grin. "Hey Ray, how are you? This must be the kid you spoke so highly of."

"Yes sir. We were hoping one of your guys could work with him on his hands today. Maybe give him a few rounds," Ray said with a slight grin, glancing over at me as he spoke.

Jimmy looked around the steamy gym and spotted a black fellow in the mirror, shadow boxing. "Hey Dean, come here," Jimmy shouted.

"You remember Ray, don't you?" Jimmy told Dean as he got within earshot.

"Sure I do," said Dean. "The kick man."

"That's him. He has this young sixteen-year-old who wants to be a champion kick-fighter someday, but ain't got a jab that could break an egg. Would you mind sparring a little with him?"

"No sir," said Dean as he turned to get his gloves and mouthpiece.

At this point the I had never boxed with a real boxer. Dean was an accomplished fighter. He had an illustrious amateur career and was now a force to be reckoned with in the light-heavyweight division. He hadn't beaten any of the top guys in the division yet, but he had hung in there with some of the best and gone the distance.

Both of us suited up. Since this was a boxing gym it didn't take long to get ready. Kickboxers would have to put on footgear, shin guards, groin protection (cups), wrap their hands, then have mouthpieces ready and headgear on. Headgear came later. In the beginning no one wore headgear.

Dean climbed into the ring as I watched. I could tell by the way he entered that it was old hat to him. He had climbed into a ring over a hundred times in his career. I followed suit and climbed in, trying to hide the fact that he was pretty nervous. There were several guys standing around the gym just watching, like they were going to see some marvelous display of boxing skill or either see Dean beat up another guy.

Hadn't all these guys seen Dean spar before? I wondered.

I held my nerves together and walked over to a corner. Not even taking the time to notice if it was red or blue. I just knew that Dean, my victim or opponent for that day, was in the other corner awaiting the bell.

"You boys ready?" Jimmy shouted, as if both of us in the ring were his sons. Dean looked over at him and nodded. Jimmy struck the bell and it rang through the gym, signifying the start of the first round. Both Dean and I moved to the center. Dean leaned over in a semi-crouch. When they met in the middle, Dean stuck out his glove to touch, which is a sign of respect, much like a bow in the martial arts. We touched gloves and we both backed up a step or so. I was scared to death, but hid it pretty well. Dean put out a couple of easy jabs to see how I would react. I brushed the jabs away with ease and thought to myself, "This guy is pretty slow for a contender."

Just when that thought crossed my mind I noticed my head was propelled back with an astronomical force. It was shocking. I had never felt that kind of power before. My eyes went instantly from looking at Dean to looking at the big ceiling fan, then back down at Dean. I realized I had just been hit with a strong, straight right hand. So much for brushing anything away with ease! Gathering my wits, I launched a series of strong jabs at Dean, which he easily deflected. So I decided to turn up the heat and launch a combination of four strong shots at the evasive boxer. None landed with any sort of authority. The end of round one ended none too soon for me, an up and coming kickboxer. Jimmy sounded the end of the three-minute round with a series of gongs on the bell and shouted: "Break, men!" Dean turned and went to his corner. In my corner, Ray was standing with a water bottle and towel. Somehow during the first round a few of the "slow jabs" must have crept through his defense and bloodied my nose. Ray wiped away the blood and took my mouthpiece out. He gave me some water and spoke in a direct, commanding tone: "Son, let's keep our hands up. This guy is quick and he surely will get to your head quicker than you can get your hands off your belly. Get 'em *up*, now!"

Breathing deep I acknowledged receiving and understanding the instructions, but between the time I came out of the corner and the time I met Dean in the center of the ring for the beginning of round two, I must have forgotten them. As a fighter I was really no match for the journeyman boxer. We weren't kicking, and kicking was my strong suit at this point. Dean was beating me to the punch pretty much eight times out of ten. As Ray kept yelling instructions to me, I would occasionally block an incoming blow and Ray would shout with encouragement, "Attaboy!" like he had never seen the other ten shots that got through my primitive defense the I was wielding.

Round two came to a close, and as I turned toward my corner, I'm sure Ray was thinking to himself, "He looks like he's done twelve rounds, not two!" As I crumpled against the corner cushion exhausted, Ray went through the systematic procedure: mouthpiece out, breathe a little, take a sip of water, swish it around, spit it out, another small sip, now listen. Ray leaned closer to my ear and said, "You're all right, champ! Just get those hands up and get more aggressive!" Jimmy shouted over to Ray, "He all right?"

Ray, not even looking back, shouted, "He's fine." Jimmy went ahead and rang the bell for the third round. I was pretty much going on all heart by this time, my body was failing but my mind overpowered the body's will to quit. I had just taken two rounds of a pretty good beating and no one knew what was holding me up. Somehow, though, when Dean and I touched gloves for round three, I seemed to be reenergized somewhat. My own pride had evidently given me a second wind and pushed me through this slump.

We bumped gloves in the center. Battered as I was, I began to pick up the pace a little and began a little more footwork than at the end of round two. I was lighter on my feet, looking for an opening and opportunity. I threw a couple of stiff jabs to test the waters. Nothing really made contact. I was a little gun shy and wanted to be sure when the time was right.

I saw an opportunity. It wasn't huge, but I knew that if there wasn't an opening I had to work to create one. Opening up with a strong double jab, I launched a straight left hand behind the ol' double. I fought southpaw in those days mostly, mainly because my best kicking leg was right, and I wanted to put that one in front—kind of a Bruce Lee philosophy. As the straight left was in motion, Dean slid just to the outside of the punch. This move was obviously one he'd done over five thousand times. As he slid outside he launched his counter, a straight right hand to the belly button. We collided in the blue corner of the ring. When the punch thrown by Dean made contact, it sank right into my stomach as my breath bellowed out like steam engine making that final puff.

I doubled over and crumpled to the mat like a wet towel. I couldn't breathe, so I simply lied on the mat gasping for air, which was so thick you could have cut it with a butter knife. Ray jumped into the ring as Dean calmly turned around and walked to the neutral corner. You could tell by Dean's nonchalant stroll back to the white corner that this was just another day at the office. Jimmy yelled up to the ring, "Is the kid all right?" Ray, again not even looking in his direction, yelled back. "Yeah, he'll be okay in a minute."

As Ray touched my crumpled body on the mat, he said, "Let's get you up and straighten you out so you can breathe." I began to rise, but started to feel nauseous. I left Ray standing in the middle of the ring and darted outside like an Olympian sprinter.

On the porch, I hung my head through the railings and began to projectile vomit. The first thing that came out was my mouthpiece and the last thing felt like my breakfast from three or four days ago. When I was finished, I hung over the railing catching my breath. Ray finally made it out to where I was and patted me on the back. Leaning over to whisper in my ear through the headgear, Ray said, "Just had the wind knocked out of you, did you?" as if no one in the building knew that. Then he walked around me hanging over the railing and down to the ground where that mouthpiece was lying in a pile of unmentionable stuff. Ray picked up the mouthpiece, washed it off with a water bottle he had been carrying around since we arrived, and looked up at me. He looked back down at the mouthpiece in his hand and then back to me. "You know, you were doing better that round. You finished three good rounds. It sure would be good if you'd go back in there and do a couple more." He said this more as a "you have to do this to save my reputation, I been bragging on you" than "if you feel like it you can do it." Ray walked back up the steps and lifted me out from between the railings, patted me on the shoulder, inserted my mouthpiece, and said, "Come on, champ, let's go get him."

"If any of you lacks wisdom, you should ask God, who gives generously to all without finding fault, and it will be given to you." (James 1:5)

Some lessons come by way of hardship or pain. I realized my shortcomings in some areas at this point, lacking some of the skills necessary to gain a world championship, so I became intentional about going and seeking it out. On that day I realized that wisdom sometimes comes at a price. One must learn from not only his or her own mistakes but also from the mistakes and lessons of others. The Bible is a big book full of stories of dos and don'ts. There are stories of people who finished strong, stuck to the course, and left a legacy to be remembered as good. Then there are stories of those who had gifts beyond compare, yet finished weak and broken in the sight of God and their fellow human beings. Ask God for wisdom, and remember that sometimes he gives it to you in an unusual manner. It could be an unanswered prayer, an unexpected letdown, the loss of a friend, or even a simple beating.

SUREFIRE STRATEGY 7: Stay in school or, if you're out, continue to pursue your education on your own. The world today is more geared toward people having college degrees than ever. I'm not saying that college is the only way to go, or that someone can't make a great living and career without a college degree, but I am saying it will give you a head start. Unless you have a technical degree such as nursing, law, or engineering, college really teaches an employer something very important about you as a candidate. It tells the employer that you are trainable and have enough discipline to stick something out long enough to finish.

SUREFIRE STRATEGY 8: Give thanks. Be grateful. An attitude of gratitude is a must for success. Every day above ground is a great day. Even when times get difficult there's always something that could be worse and something to be thankful for. Begin each day with a blessing count and end each day in silent reflection.

SUREFIRE STRATEGY 9: Remember you are who you associate with. A man once told me that you are plus or minus 20 percent of who you hang out with. He's probably not far off. If you want to grow, you have to be around people who facilitate that growth. Spending time with quality individuals is paramount. These types of quality people are willing to tell you the hard stuff. The hard stuff is the truth. If you're veering off course, you'll need someone who loves you enough and is sharp enough to see it and let you know. People don't normally just push you off a cliff, but they will gently nudge you until it's too late. So hang out with the right kind of people.

CHAPTER 4

AT THE FIGHTS WITH A FRIEND

My heart raced as I tried to regulate my breathing. I was wracked with pain, but the nurse told my mom I could have no more pain medication for another two hours. Sleep was the farthest thing from my mind, even though I'd been awake since emerging from recovery some eight hours earlier. You'd think that with all the high-powered pain meds I would have been able to doze just to pass the time, but no, time was moving at a crawl. The only thing I could hear was the pounding of my heart and the forced breathing through my clenched teeth.

How could this have happened to an up-and-coming athlete with all the ability I had gained at this point? My dreams were set in stone at age thirteen, and I knew God had placed me on this path—a path to become a world champion in a young sport. Everything was laid out perfectly, or so I had thought.

Now all I could remember was a nurse anesthetist asking me to count backward from five, and then I remembered rolling on a gurney down the hall, opening my eyes briefly to see my Dad leaning over and smiling at me. You know you can always count on your dad to be there when you most need him, but it was my mom who was staying the night tonight. She was lying on a little ledge under the window in this fourth-floor room. She would lie quietly, trying to sleep, until either the nurse came in to check on me or I would jump up and stumble across the room, usually tearing the IV from my arm, blood pulsing from the wound. Several times during the night my mom would call the nurse in because I would get somewhat violent with my movements and start groaning. My mouth was wired tightly shut so the nurse would come in to check my vitals often. Keeping one's mouth closed in this wired state causes the body to run a low-grade fever. Coupled with the pain of fresh surgery, this tends to cause people to go slightly crazy.

The sun rose the next day on my Mom sitting up on the ledge she had attempted to sleep, just staring at me. Tears gently rolled down her face when the nurse came in for her morning check. She looked over at my Mom, obviously in emotional pain to see her son suffering so. The nurse made a little small talk as she did her procedures. I drifted off to sleep for the first time in about thirty hours.

"Is he going to rest some now?" my mother asked the nurse.

"He should, ma'am. The first night after this type of surgery is always the roughest. It's a pretty painful procedure and he had a couple of bad breaks in his lower mandible."

"I think I'm going to run home for a while. I need to do a few errands and check on my other son," said my Mom.

"He'll be fine, ma'am. You go ahead. We'll call you if there's an issue," the nurse replied as she finished putting some medication in my IV.

Once I had finally drifted off to sleep, my Mom left for some much-needed time away from the hospital. My baby brother, who is eight years younger than I, would be getting home from school shortly. A neighbor was doing the pickup duty during this time.

I somehow slept relatively soundly considering that I had my mouth wired shut and a fever of 102. The pain meds flowed freely. I began to get a little restless in the hospital bed, my mind racing almost as fast as my pulse. I began to hallucinate that I was walking down a long corridor toward a light at the end.

The light appeared from a distance to be an opening into a large arena of some kind, like you see in *Rocky* as he's entering the arena to fight Apollo Creed. In this dream I was walking down this corridor, geared up to fight the kickboxing match of my life. Finally, after years of training, I had a twelve-round world championship fight waiting at the end of this long tunnel. There were five people walking along side me. For some reason I wasn't sure who these five guys were, but I knew they were part of my team. I knew they had helped me prepare for this event in some way. Each guy was hugely important in my life and career, but in this half dream–half reality state I just wasn't sure how.

The end of the tunnel was approaching, and we all moved steadily forward. I was bouncing to an inner beat, a confident beat only heard by me and the other five with me moving down this path. When we arrived at the end of the tunnel, I just stopped and stood for a moment, looking across hundreds of people gathered around the boxing ring ready for the upcoming battle. I saw in the ring my opponent, his corner men, and the referee. The ring announcer was even standing there holding the microphone, where he had just announced, "And in the blue corner …"

In an instant everyone was gone. The people I had seen screaming my name, the opponent in the ring staying warm in preparation for the upcoming battle—all were gone. The ring announcer had vanished, the microphone still hanging with just a little swing back and forth. I was somehow now left standing at the end of this long tunnel with no one around, I was all alone. The seats of the huge arena were empty. The boxing ring stood in the middle, with no opponent there. I could still smell that arena smell, stale popcorn, spilt beer on the floor. The ring was still lit as if the fight was going to take place. The judge's tables were still in place, and all looked as if there was going to be a huge event shortly.

Now I stood alone at the end of the tunnel, just staring at the chairs, wondering where all these people could have gone in an instant. Then in a ringside seat, right next to the blue corner, a spotlight shone on a man with long hair. The man seem to have no idea the show was probably not going to happen. His brown hair glistened in the spotlight, which spilled over into the first row of blue corner seats.

I looked down at my hands where the blue gloves were laced tightly, ready for battle. In an instant the gloves were gone and now I stood barehanded, in my hospital gown of all things, staring at an empty ring with some strange long-haired fellow the only soul other than me in this huge arena. I stood still, not knowing what to do next. For some reason I felt drawn toward that blue corner where that man was sitting.

I thought to myself, "I did have those blue gloves on, so maybe I should go on over to the blue corner." All the nervous energy that had been racing through my veins as it does before a competition was somehow gone. In its place was an unusual calm and peace. The pain of the hospital room and gloom which had surrounded me was now gone and replaced with an expectant jubilation. My mouth, which had been wired tightly shut, was no longer bound. It was as pain-free as ever now, with no restrictions.

I realized I was motionless, even though I had decided to go to the blue corner. It was as if my feet had stood there so long that roots had begun to form from my soles to the concrete floor. Then I made a conscious effort to pick up one foot and put it in front of the other, in order to gain some forward momentum. It was a good hundred yards to the blue corner seats, and I enjoyed the gentle slope of the aisle, which allowed my sluggish feet to pick up steam. As I grew closer to the man sitting in the front row I felt an overwhelming sense of warmth. The type of warmth you used to feel when your mother cooked those special cookies on a winter's day, and after they were finished she left the oven door open, because she didn't want to waste the heat. So, as a little child, you would go stand in front of the oven until all the warmth that came from the oven, along with a little mama love, dissipated into the small kitchen.

I finally made it to the front row, but the man was not acknowledging my presence. This man actually looked as though he was watching an ongoing match in the ring. Standing in my hospital gown and bedroom slippers, I glanced into the ring to make sure I wasn't missing anything. As strange as this whole scene was, one could never be too careful.

To steady myself I held on to each seat as I made my way to the stranger. As I passed each seat I would look down and see the ascending numbers on the seat backs. Forty seats were in each row, and I was at that moment standing beside seat 1A. I walked slowly past 2A, 3A, 4A ... and finally reached 35A. I stopped, expecting the man to turn toward me and say something. He continued staring into the empty ring, watching the imaginary match or something. I thought to myself, "It must be a pretty boring kickboxing match: this guy is just sitting there with his legs crossed, kind of nodding along." The seated stranger had an interested grin on his face as he peered into the ring. A proud grin, maybe that of a father as he watched his son win an award or graduate from school.

Reluctantly, I decided to sit down beside the stranger, hoping I could see whatever he was watching in the ring. I figured he was in this crazy dream, so I'd better get some entertainment out of it. I sat down on the man's left and crossed my legs in a similar fashion as he, hoping I'd at least be acknowledged. We sat side by side for what seemed like an eternity, but must have really only been four or five minutes.

"That was a good fight," the long-haired stranger said, finally breaking the silence of the big arena.

"A good fight? I didn't see anything," I quickly replied.

The long-haired stranger shook his head and said, "I figured you didn't. That's the problem with you boys, I could put it right in front of you and you wouldn't see it."

"Well, there's nothing there!" I snorted back. "Besides, who are you anyway and how can you see what's going on in there? You look like a crazy old bum to me."

"I've been called worse, son. 'Old' isn't that bad, but 'bum' I wouldn't really agree with."

"I'm sorry, sir, I'm just in a poor mood right now. You see, I should be in there, doing my thing."

"In where?" asked the stranger.

"In there, in the boxing ring. You see, I've had this goal since I was a kid to be a world-champion kickboxer," I continued, slightly irritated.

"You're still a kid. Can you not see that you are there now? Who do you think I was just watching?"

"What! You have to be crazy old man. That ring was empty—about as empty as your head, apparently," I said in a sarcastic tone.

"The ring may have seemed empty to you, son, but to me you are very much there. You see, the problem with you humans is that you lack foresight and faith. If a man uses his imagination properly and has faith, the future can be very much the present."

"Man, you are talking in riddles now," I said disrespectfully. "Have you been drinking or something?"

"No, son. I've turned water into wine, but I don't make it a habit of drinking it," the man said.

"So you're telling me you're some kind of fortuneteller or magician or something?" I asked.

"I've been called many of those and more, son. Some people call me this and that and some people don't even call me at all, which really hurts my feelings."

"You're a dream dude, how can you have feelings?" I said spitefully.

"Oh, I have feelings, son, and even more since the accident. I felt everything you humans feel: the good, the bad, and more," the man said.

"Accident? What do you mean accident?" I asked.

"Well, I like to call it an accident because it's painful to think *my* father could desire me to go through what I did. But I understand now, whereas when the accident was happening I didn't. I just knew I had to do what my father wished. You know it's wrong to disobey your father, don't you?"

"Yes, I know," I answered in a rhetorical tone. "I have great parents and I try to do everything they say. But what kind of accident are you talking about? You talk about it like it really transformed your life."

The man turned and looked dead at me as if he could see right down to my soul. He gave me a feeling of contentment and healing unlike anything I'd ever felt.

The man stared at me for a minute without speaking. I just couldn't look away. I was in total awe of the man's calmness and total control over the situation. The man's piercing blue eyes seem to melt away any tension in the air. At a time in my life when I felt so out of control, I couldn't help but draw closer to this man, whoever he was, who seemed to have his act so together. The man reached over and put his hand on my hand and said: "You see, son, a long time ago my father had an idea. Not just any idea, but an idea that would not only change your life but everyone's life. And when I say everyone, I mean *everyone*. He started his whole idea out with a plan that, unbeknownst to me at the time, would be changed dramatically from what I originally thought it to be. My father shares everything with me and my roommate; however, there are a few items he keeps to himself. He has his reasons, you know."

"Wait a minute!" I shouted, I couldn't take much more of his nonsense. "So you and your dad live in a big house and you've got a roommate who knows everything you know about your so-called father's plans?"

"Yes, son, just the three of us."

"And how long have you and your father and your friend been living in this house?" I asked.

"Let's just say since way before you were born. In fact, I remember when you were born and even before that," answered the old man.

"Okay, this is getting ridiculous. You brought me here where I was supposed to be fighting for the world championship and you make everyone disappear. You somehow pulled me out of the hospital I was in and you fixed my mouth … what's going on?"

"Calm down, son. You'll understand in due time. You see, sometimes as you're going along in life things appear to be the way they should. Then, because you live in a fallen world …" He hesitated, then said: "Let's not get ahead of ourselves. Back to my story, so you'll understand better. You see, the original plans put into motion by father were perfect. He is the Master Craftsman, you know? In fact, His plan would have not been thwarted were it not for this one guy. You see, this guy gets great pleasure from messing things up. He gets in the middle of Father and his family quite a bit."

"What's this guy's problem?" I asked the stranger.

"He and my father had a falling out, son. Many years ago, this guy thought it would be great to try and imitate my father. He tried to boss people around on my father's job site and got a little too big for his britches. Father didn't see that as acceptable. That guy had gotten a little haughty, and Father told him he had to go live by himself. So this guy moved on with a few of his friends and is living in a different neighborhood."

"Interesting," I said, as I settled down into a seat.

"Yeah, it is. But the good thing about it is that because my father loved you, me, and the rest of his family, he made sure we all could have time with him."

"Your father loves me too? I don't understand," I said to the man in a perplexed tone.

"You don't need to. See, that's the beauty of it. All you have to do is believe. Son, you've come a long way on belief, but for some reason now, you're doubting what you're here for. Your path was laid out a long time ago. You know, in

<u>Psalm 139, verses thirteen</u> and fourteen? It says 'For you created my inmost being; you knit me together in my mother's womb. I praise you because I am fearfully and wonderfully made.' See, son, you are wonderfully made. So much so that God couldn't stand to see you sin and willed to eternally suffer for your sins. So He sent His only Son to take that punishment for you."

As the stranger spoke, I couldn't help but watch his features. This man looked as though he'd been through some difficult times, yet he carried a self-evident peace about him. I noticed scars on the guy's face as though he'd been in a real fight, with no gloves. As I shifted my eyes from the man's face to different parts of his body it occurred to me that this dream was more real than any I'd ever had. The old man reached out and grabbed my hand, and as he did so, I saw awful-looking marks in his hands.

"Son, you don't have to fight everything. Some things require no battle. They just come naturally if you'd let 'em."

"Well, if you are who I think you are, you've got a lot of explaining to do!" I shouted at the man in anger. "I was on a winning streak, knocking people out every match and on track to be a world champion, and you let me get a broken jaw."

"I *let* you, son? How could I let you? You're the one with the training and should have blocked that shot," he replied.

"Yeah, you're right about that. Now I'm wired up and can't eat or talk, and definitely can't train for a long time. I may not even be able to fight again. After you put me on this path … and now? What a cruel sense of humor you have."

"You may be a little angry now, because you don't understand, but I never allowed this just to make a joke out of you or your dreams. Father would never do that."

I glared intensely at him. "Well, how come he gave me all these big ideas of being the best, competing at the top of sport, but then says, 'Oh, wait a minute, maybe I made a mistake. Let's take you in another direction. Let's get you hurt, so you'll just give up. Yeah, how about if he doesn't eat or talk for eight weeks or so—that should crush him!"

"Son, you've got it all wrong. Father wouldn't do that. You see, his plans are higher than your plans. You as humans only see a glimpse of what is to be. You can't see the entire picture. There's no way. Only Father, well ... and me and his roommate see the whole picture."

"The whole picture? How can you say that you're just an old man at a fight? You've got to be crazy," I said in that same sarcastic tone looking down at the floor now.

"Son, Father is not vindictive. He does nothing without a reason. His reasons are always for His good. 'And we know that in all things God works for the good of those who love Him, who have been called according to His purpose.' Romans 8:28."

"There you go again, throwing in these stupid sayings. What are you, some kind of Confucius or something?" I said.

"No son, I am no Confucius. Those are from a famous book my Father wrote."

Smirking, I said, "So your father is a famous author too. Who is he, Mark Twain?"

"No, son. It works like this. Father has a plan laid out for all His children, even before they are born. He lays out these plans, carefully putting all the pieces into a proper order that only He could. Then He waits."

"Waits on what?" I yelled impatiently.

"He waits to see if each person will look to Him to see the plan that is laid before them. See, there are millions of plans laid out before millions of people, but only a small percentage of those folks actually care to seek the Father and see what He has to offer."

"What about when I thought it was His plan and now it appears I was wrong? Why would He lead me in one direction if He is 'all knowing' as people say, and then wait until I'm pretty far down the path and change His mind without my knowing?" I asked as I sat back down on a chair a few spaces away from the man and put my head in his hands.

The scarred man rose from his seat and walked over to me, by this time I was in tears, totally confused. He put his hand on my shoulder and sat down beside me. Leaning close, he said, "Son, God is not capricious in nature. He would not lead you down a false path or give you a path to follow without equipping you with the tools to follow that particular path. I know that right now you may not feel that way, but it's true, son. And you know what they say about truth?"

I interrupted quickly, "Yeah, yeah ... the truth shall set you free!"

"No, son. That's only half the truth. Many people are a victim of misquoting Dad's famous book or even saying pieces of sentences in the book. That's one of them, for sure. "'Jesus therefore said to those Jews that had believed him,' If ye abide in my word, [then] are ye truly my disciples; and ye shall know the truth, and the truth shall make you free.'" (John 8:32). You see son, you have to know the truth of Jesus, not just the truth of anything. This truth is very specific. The truth is about Me."

I began to weep bitterly with my head in my hands. "You love me too, don't you?"

"Yes sir, more than you'll ever know. Father loves you, and so does our other friend," the man said. I arose and He stood beside me, and we stared at the ring together. Tears were still streaming down my face. We stood for several seconds, maybe even minutes, and then I spoke up: "Maybe I shouldn't push this world champ thing so hard. Maybe I should look at other paths. It really doesn't matter if I'm not doing what the Father wants, does it?"

The man kicked his feet back and forth for a second, and then spoke up: "You know what I was watching when I brought you here from the hospital room?"

I shook my head as if to say it really didn't matter. Of course, I had no idea.

"I was watching your big match," the man went on. "You, son! I was watching you—and you were doing quite well, by the way. I'd say you were winning going into the eleventh round."

"What?" I exclaimed, surprised.

"Do you think Father would have led you this way if He didn't expect you to finish? He gave you all this tenacity, not necessarily talent, and He expects you to accomplish what was placed in your heart."

"Really? But I thought maybe this was His way of saying 'Hold up now, I've got another plan.'"

"Son, sometimes the father puts some obstacles in the way to test you a little. He never said easy was part of the plan. Read the book. Sometimes he just wants to see how serious you are. You'll never know how many people in their lifetime get to a point like you have and just give up. Then they never really realize their fullest potential."

I just stood, staring at him. We stood motionless only a few chairs down from where we had first spoken. The man gave me a big hug. As he squeezed me tightly, a feeling of comfort and warmth ran all up and down my body unlike anything I've ever experienced. Then the man pulled back, looked deep into my eyes, and said softly, "Now go get 'em, champ!"

SUREFIRE STRATEGY 10: Be by yourself. Learn to be alone. Learn to sit quietly in a room with no noise and just listen. This is a great time to practice your deep breathing exercises. Western society places little value on breathing exercises. You can study breathing from several cultures, or even theater and voice. Aim for a good abdominal diaphragmatic breathing, where the breath gets way down in the abdominal region. This breathing, combined with good visualization, can be a huge benefit to anyone. Sitting by yourself can often help you realize who you're sitting with.

SUREFIRE STRATEGY 11: Cry sometimes. Don't be afraid to let your emotions out, but learn to control them. You always need to control your emotions so they serve you and not the other way around. Go see a good movie that moves you emotionally. My father used to call those sappy movies tearjerkers. A good cry helps purify the soul.

SUREFIRE STRATEGY 12: Fail forward. In life you are going to mess up. You are sometimes going to fall short of your goal. Someone told me once that goals are not always meant to be reached; they simply serve as something to aim at. That has some truth to it. If you aim at nothing, that's what you'll get every time. No one sets a goal without intentions of reaching it, but if you set your mark too high and fall a little short it's better than not trying. If you *do* fail, don't sit around and lick your wounds. You may need a day or so of mourning the failure, but then you must pick yourself up, learn what mistakes you've made, and then push on.

CHAPTER 5

FINDING GUIDANCE

I woke up in my hospital bed with a nurse on one side and a nun on the other. I knew I was in a Catholic hospital but thought nothing of it. By this time I had been through so much I could have been in any kind of hospital and not known the difference.

The nurse finished checking vitals and my IV hook-up, and left the room as stealthily as she had entered. The nun stood there as if she was waiting for something. She began to ask a question. I realized she was speaking a foreign language and I didn't understand a word of what she was saying. I thought maybe she was speaking Spanish, but in the groggy state I was in, I really couldn't tell what language was coming from this white-clothed person. Finally, realizing that she wasn't getting through and that I couldn't open my mouth anyway, she put her hands together to signify prayer and said, "Yes, yes?"

I knew she wasn't going to leave, so I nodded. The nun grabbed my hand and bowed her head. I looked at her for a second, and then bowed my head as well. She began to pray in her language. It seemed poetic to me as she spoke, almost angelic. I didn't know what she was saying, but knew that it was important and that she was talking to God, so I did my best to be attentive.

I heard her utter an "Amen," and then she looked up at me and smiled broadly. I nodded to thank her for her kindness. She said another sentence or two in Spanish, smiled real big, and swiftly departed. Watching her leave I was quite confused. All I had experienced was jumbled together in my head and it was difficult for me to distinguish reality from a medically-induced dream. I looked over and saw my pulse and blood pressure on the monitor, so deduced that the praying nun had been real and I was really in this hospital. The pain began to work its way back into my head and mouth.

Fidgeting around in my bed, I saw a Bible in the drawer to my right. It looked like one of those hotel Gideon Bibles. I thought to himself, "Do the Gideons do hotels and hospitals?" Reaching over to the side table, I picked it up. Not the first time I'd ever picked one up, but the first time I'd picked one up with real intent of getting something out of it. I finagled the book through the wires and cords from machines, found a flat place on the bed, and propped myself up on my elbow so I could read. I really didn't know what he was looking for; I just knew that after the time spent in the arena with that old fight fan there was something I needed to see. I opened it up and it fell to the ninety-first chapter of Psalms.

1 He who dwells in the shelter of the Most High will rest in the shadow of the Almighty. **2** I will say of the LORD, "He is my refuge and my fortress, my God, in whom I trust." **3** Surely he will save you from the fowler's snare and from the deadly pestilence. **4** He will cover you with his feathers, and under his wings you will find refuge; his faithfulness will be your shield and rampart. **5** You will not fear the terror of night, nor the arrow that flies by day, **6** nor the pestilence that stalks in the darkness, nor the plague that destroys at midday. **7** A thousand may fall at your side, ten thousand at your right hand, but it will not come near you. **8** You will only observe with your eyes and see the punishment of the wicked. **9** If you make the Most High your dwelling—even the LORD, who is my refuge—**10** then no harm will befall you, no disaster will come near your tent. **11** For he will command his angels concerning you to guard you in all your ways; **12** they will lift you up in their hands, so that you will not strike your foot against a stone. **13** You will tread upon the lion and the cobra; you will trample the great lion and the serpent. **14** "Because he loves me," says the LORD, "I will rescue him; I will protect him, for he acknowledges my name. **15** He will call upon me, and I will answer him; I will be with him in trouble, I will deliver him and honor him. **16** With long life will I satisfy him and show him my salvation."

I read the chapter to myself and thought about what this had to do with the predicament I found myself in. I wished the old man at the ring was with me so he could shed some light on this written word. I felt a little groggy so I laid the Bible down by my bedside and laid my head on the pillow.

I was able to go home the next day. When I arrived home, I headed into my room. Everything was as I had left it. The posters on the wall, the karate certificates … everything was the same. Even though I was now legally a man and registered for the draft, I stayed with my parents for a time. I shuffled through some old magazines in my desk drawer, looking for an old Ringside catalogue I'd received in the mail before the accident. I made humming noises as I moved everything in the drawer from one side to the other. With my mouth still wired shut, my next six or so weeks were going to be a long hungry time. I found the Ringside book and sat down on the bed. I began flipping the pages rapidly until I came to the headgear section. I knew there was one in there with a faceguard on it. I wanted one that would cover my jaw area and still allow me to spar. I found it and laid it open on his desk. I knew God had put me on a path to be a champ and I needed some extra protection during these healing weeks after my mouth was unwired.

In life things are not always as they seem. God sends us into this world with ambitions and a will. He wants our will to align with His. Sometimes in His all-knowing nature He tests the fortitude of our dreams. He isn't going to let you hit the mark without having you grow during the process. Each step along the way is a classroom, and it's up to you to listen to what the Teacher has to teach.

SUREFIRE STRATEGY 13: Trust people. This is scary for many people, and no one can say you'll never get burned, but to build trust and understand faith one must trust first. Faith is not something we believe, it's something we do. Sticking your neck out is sometimes scary, but overall you'll find that the large majority of people want to be trusted just like you. It's the law of reciprocation. To be trusted you must first trust.

SUREFIRE STRATEGY 14: Be faithful and true. This is not just being true to your spouse, your friends, and your country. Be faithful to your church, your work, or any organization you've pledged your support to. Many times people join an organization when things are great. They are excited about the new affiliation, but something may happen in the organization with which they feel uneasy with. Then they think about jumping ship and moving to a different similar organization. In the martial arts business we have something called "school jumpers." These are students who come in, join up, and then in a month or so decide what we do wasn't what they wanted, so they move down the street to the next martial arts place. What we do may not be for everybody, but if you don't stick with it for an extended period of time you'll never gain any benefits. School jumpers usually never become good at martial arts because they're too busy jumping around.

SUREFIRE STRATEGY 15: Keep your promises. Zig Ziglar said it well: "If your word is no good, then you're no good." In life you'll make commitments and promises, and some of them will be hard to keep. When they are hard to keep, the true material you're made of shows through. You can't just give up. My father says that a man must stand by his word, even if it hurts. Sometimes it will. You may make a business deal that doesn't turn out quite as well as you had anticipated. You may be having marital problems and threatening to walk away. It's not about you being happy. This whole life isn't about you. Happiness is a choice, just like getting up this morning is a choice. Choose to stick it out.

Psalm 15:4 "In whose eyes a reprobate is despised, But who honoreth them that fear Jehovah; He that sweareth to his own hurt, and changeth not."

CHAPTER 6

OPPORTUNITY KNOCKS

I had now won several matches and beaten some of the best in the game. At the time, I was ranked the eighth-best kickboxer in the world and was looking to move up. My jaw had healed well. During the healing process and post-operation visits the doctors had found I had wisdom teeth growing at an angle, which were putting pressure my jaw bone and making it prone to breaks. Not what a fighter wants to have! After the extraction of all four wisdom teeth and an extra year or so of healing I was now ready to continue this climb.

At this point in my fighting career I'd not yet had my endurance tested. I had knocked out most of my opponents early in the fight, and had never had to go into the deep water of later rounds. I was traveling quite a bit, going wherever I could spar and get in a workout. Much of my training was back at the old boxing gym where Dean had knocked the puke out of me years before. Ray was always there, pushing me as I trained. I still trained at the karate school I had grown up in whenever I could. I couldn't get that out of my system no matter how much I trained.

He received a phone call one night from a promoter in New Hampshire. This promoter was trying to get a hometown guy a shot at a world title and was flying in Dale "Sunshine" Frye to defend his world lightweight title against Steve Demenchuk.

"Hi," the promoter said. "This is Tom Young from Manchester, New Hampshire. We are trying to fill an undercard for a world title show in our town and wanted to see if you'd be willing to do a five rounder against the number-three contender."

I held my breath with excitement as the man spoke.

"Yes sir!" I answered, barely letting the promoter finish his sentence.

"Great!" replied Tom. "However, there are a couple of things you need to know before you say yes. One, there's not a lot of money in it for you—we're paying the champion such a big purse our money is spent—but it will allow you an opportunity to get your ranking up … maybe even to number one. We can only pay you five hundred bucks, and no travel. I'll give you some per diem money but I can't swing the plane ticket for you and your trainer."

"That doesn't matter, Tom," I replied. "I'll figure out a way to get there. I may have to walk, but I'll be there to fight the guy."

"Okay, then. I'll send you the contract. Please sign it and get it back to me as soon as you can. We want to get this wrapped up," Tom said.

I was actually going to get a shot. A shot that could catapult me straight to the number-one slot.

Early next morning I gave Ray a call. I left him a message that I had a fight coming up and needed some help. Ray called back that afternoon and confirmed he'd be willing to go and help in the corner. The training period was to begin.

Being one hundred percent healed and ready to take over the world, everything went well in training. I was able to get plenty of sparring, road work, and all the training that goes into being a champion. I put two plane tickets from his home town to Manchester, NH on a credit card for me and Ray. Now we were ready. Finally the day came. As the wheels touched down in Manchester, both of us were anticipating the great match to come.

It was Saturday, time to go to the venue for the event. The fights started at seven that evening, but all fighters had to be on site by four p.m. in order to go through the athletic commission's checks and physicals and the rules meeting prior to the first bell. I was feeling strong so I walked into the convention center exuding confidence, as if I'd had already won.

The physicals went well and the rules meeting went well. We finished and went over to the bleachers to rest a bit before the show. The arena was enormous, so we went to a corner where we could be out of the way yet get a straight view of the ring. Our bout was sixth on the card of ten bouts so we had a little time before we had to go through the ritual of wrapping hands, putting on equipment, applying

Vaseline to the face and body to make sure blows slid off without cutting, and other particulars.

Ray noticed the promoter of the show walking briskly toward us as we sat in the corner. Ray nudged me and said, "Looks like Tom the promoter is headed this way."

"Wonder what he wants," I replied.

Tom greeted us cordially, but with an obvious question looming in his mind. "Everything going well?" he asked Ray.

"Yes sir, we're all set to go, just waiting on our time," Ray said to Tom.

"I got a favor," Tom said. "I had two fighters pull out on me just now, and I wanted to see if you guys would be willing to do an eight rounder instead of five? That would fill in some time on the card before the main event."

Ray looked at me. I quickly gave an enthusiastic nod. "Sure, we'll do as many as you need," Ray said.

"Wow, thanks guys," Tom said. "I was looking at being short tonight, but you guys helped me out. Thanks again." He hurried off back to ringside to make sure all changes were noted with the officials.

We both looked at each other when Tom walked away. Ray immediately said, "You're ready for eight just like you're ready for five, don't worry about it."

This change had my mind racing. I'd never done that many rounds before in a real show. I knew conditioning was the key to any fight. Sure, I'd sparred in the gym that many and more, but when you add the pressure of the crowd, the nervous energy of an important fight, and the fact that you're fighting a ranked contender, that makes a huge difference. I tried to control my mind. I thought to myself, "I wanted to step in to a different league, the big league, and this is as good a time as any. Surely I can do three more rounds. I may not even need five rounds. I should be able to take this guy out before that. I just need to calm down and have faith in my training."

Ray looked up at me and said, "It's about time to get to the dressing room—they're fixin' to get started. Let's go wrap those hands."

The athletic commission came by to check the tape on my hands and gave me the gloves. Ray had to slide them on one at a time and carefully lace them, making sure to skin them back as best he could. Skinning the glove back is a way to tie a set of boxing gloves in which you pull the strings over the leather as you tie them in order to tighten the leather across the hand and knuckles. This gives you a slight advantage when you make good contact with a punch. The leather pulled taut across the knuckles makes it more likely to cut an opponent. It's not illegal, and every fighter usually does it if they know about it.

Now that I was gloved up, I stood just outside the dressing room with my fight apparel on and gloves taped. I bounced rhythmically as I waited for the announcer to call me to my corner. Usually a fighter had at least two corner men, but due to having to purchase our own plane tickets, I could only bring Ray, and that was fine with me. We'd done it before. Finally the previous fight was over by decision. I was up next. Since I was the visiting fighter the announcer called me out first.

The ring announcer growled through the loud speaker: "In the blue corner, weighing in at one hundred and eighty-five pounds, with a professional record of thirteen wins and one loss, with eight wins by way of knockout … from Lyman, South Carolina …".

I commenced to jog toward the ring, with Ray leading the way. Ray climbed the steps to the blue corner while I waited behind him donning the black robe with Kevin "Hurricane" Hudson sewn across my back. Ray got up to the ring and put his foot and knee between the ropes to let me in. I took a short jog around the perimeter of the ring as if to say, "I own this place" to my opponent, who was waiting to be called to the ring. Finishing my warm up jog, I settled back to the blue corner and waited for my opponent to be called in. Then the announcer's voice reverberated through the microphone: "And in the red corner, weighing in at one hundred and eighty-nine pounds … with a record of twelve wins and zero losses, with ten wins coming by way of knockout … John Mazulli!"

The crowd cheered deafeningly. They were rooting for their hometown boy. I glanced out of the ring from the corner and saw my opponent walking briskly toward the ring. This guy had on a green robe and red gloves, and I thought to myself how those red gloves didn't match that green robe. Then I had to get my head back in check. The fact that my opponent must have been from Ireland originally wasn't important now. He's was from Long Island, New York now.

As he entered the ring, Ray took off my black robe and made sure I had a sip of water, then inserted my mouthpiece. Looking in my eyes, he slapped me in the midsection area to keep me pumped and alert. "You got this," he said.

The referee called us to the center. We gazed into each other's eyes, trying to read the other's heart. The referee gave his commands and ended with: "Protect yourself at all times, touch gloves, and come out at the bell." We bumped gloves firmly as a sign of respect. I backed up, keeping his eyes on Mazulli across the ring. Ray put his fist up when I reached the corner for a bump and yelled, "You got this!"

The bell rang and both Mazulli and I approached the middle of the ring with hands up. I noticed immediately that Mazulli was right handed, so I started things off by slamming a hard round kick into his stomach. Mazulli blocked it pretty easily. I always started all my fights off with a good strong kick. This was an attitude adjustment right off the bat. The opponent always knew, no matter what happened in the fight, I could kick him hard. After that initial kick the round was pretty even. We both attempted a flurry of techniques periodically, with little success. The first round is usually a feeling-out round, to get the feel of the energy of that new person in the ring with you.

The bell rang signaling the end of the round. We backed up out of range and headed back to our designated corners. Ray was waiting at the corner for me. Ray guided me down on the stool and took out my mouthpiece. Ray held the mouthpiece over the spit bucket, washed it out with his water bottle, and looked at me intently.

"How you feeling?" he shouted over the roar of the crowd.

"Good," I shouted back, panting.

"You got this, son. Just make sure to keep your hands up. This guy's got a strong right hand. He's waiting on you to kick and then counter," Ray said as he gave me a sip of water. I nodded and bit down on the fresh mouthpiece. The referee yelled, "Seconds out!"

Ray quickly exited the ring, removed the stool, and wiped up the excess water from the floor of the ring.

We met in the middle of the ring. Muzilli came out strong, with a good combination, but making minimal contact. I was light on my feet and evaded most shots thrown by the veteran. About halfway through the round I was a little weary. Losing focus for a split second, I caught a strong overhand right to the head. I went reeling back and the crowd roared louder than ever. The second round ended with me playing defense and moving backwards. The bell sounded the end of the second round. Both of us turned to go to our perspective corners.

Ray had the stool ready, and was a bit concerned. I was a little gassed after this round. The nerves and pressure had wreaked havoc on my physical state. I sat on the stool and Ray sprayed water on my face to wake me up and get me back focused. He removed my mouthpiece and said, "You all right, son. This is what we came for. Suck it up and keep those hands high. We are headed into round three."

The whistle blew and the referee shouted, "Seconds out!" Ray patted me on the leg and said, "Let's go get him." I rose from the stool and pushed my mouthpiece in. The bell rang for the beginning of the third round. The referee gave the command: "Fight."

Both my opponent and I were a little calmer now. We slowly began to move in a counterclockwise direction, sizing up the other for an attack. Muzulli pawed a couple of jabs out at me, feeling for an opening in my defense, but I easily brushed away the incoming blows. I held my hands high, but my energy level was running low. My mind wavered between "I gotta win this round" and "I'm not sure I can make it five rounds, much less eight." The round was pretty even up until about thirty seconds before the bell. We had somehow gotten tangled up in the middle of the ring. We both had thrown a series of punches and the other blocked, then stepped in to counter, but it was unsuccessful and we just sort of hugged each other in the middle of the ring. The referee jumped into the middle of us and shouted, "Break!" We backed up as the referee stepped between. Once we were separated far enough apart he clapped his hands together and yelled, "Fight!"

I saw an opportunity, a weak link in the Muzulli chain, so when the referee commanded the battle to continue I quickly closed the gap and popped off two strong jabs and a straight left hand. I shuffled forward on both techniques to close the distance between us. Muzulli blocked the first two jabs with his lead hand, but allowed the straight left to squeak by his defenses. The left made pretty good contact with Muzulli's chin, rocking the Italian's head back and forcing him to drop his right guard a bit. I followed the straight left with my signature rear leg round kick. My back leg went straight from the floor, over the right guard of Muzulli and struck Muzulli about the lower ear, in the neck area. As my foot hit the floor I was somewhoat stunned that my three piece attack worked. Muzulli was hurt! He stumbled back toward the neutral corner and I pursued. I followed Muzulli and began to unleash a series of finishing punches. The referee, seeing these damaging blows adding up on Muzulli's already dazed state, jumped between us, yelling, "Break!"

He looked at me as he got in the middle of us and pointed to the neutral corner. Excited to see the results of my efforts, I watched the referee begin the count as I moved toward the white corner. The referee looked intently at Muzulli, trying to assess his ability to continue the battle. Each referee takes a vow to put the fighter's safety first and ensure that no fighter takes too much abuse and is permanently injured. The referee reached six, seven, then eight. He looked at Muzulli and said, "Walk to me."

This is the standard test referees use to assess a fighter's state: they watch a hurt fighter walk to them after they've been rattled pretty good. If the fighter steps in a few post holes as he's walking to the referee, this tells the referee that this guy isn't prepared to finish the fight. If he walks straight, looking the referee in the eyes without wobbling, then he's probably all right for the moment.

Muzulli pushed himself from the corner pad and attempted to walk straight to the referee, but apparently the cobwebs created by that strong rear leg kick to the neck were too much, distorting his vision and stability. He wobbled toward the ref in almost a drunken state. The referee grabbed Muzulli and hugged him, waving his arm wildly in the air, signaling a stoppage. I had conquered my demons of self-doubt and beaten a top-ranked contender by a third-round knockout!

Sometimes in life the battle plan is compromised by a change of environment or a change of battle parameters.

This is when God steps in for you and gives you the strength to fight the battle strong and courageous. That day there was no way I could have done eight rounds. Nerves and excitement had probably taken five rounds out of me before I even stepped in the ring. I was inexperienced compared to my opponent that day, but God stepped in and gave me the ability to be a little more skilled than my opponent. Often in life you can't judge a man on his experience level but on his performance. As a fighter I had the faith of a giant that day that one day I would be champion, and that faith—the evidence of something not seen—pushed me to victory.

As Hebrews 11:30 says: It was by faith that the people of Israel marched around Jericho for seven days, and the walls came crashing down. It was by faith that Rahab the prostitute was not destroyed with the people in her city who refused to obey God. For she had a friendly welcome to the spies.

As humans we often lack the faith to accomplish what God has laid before us. Even in the bleakest times, when your world is crumbling and the path has become crooked and bumpy, you have to remember, "trust in the Lord with all your heart, and do not lean on your own understanding. Think about him in all your ways and He will make your path smooth and straight. (Pro. 3:5). It's not God that stops us from hitting the mark, it's us, and our lack of faith.

SUREFIRE STRATEGY 16: Keep a journal. I have found this very fulfilling, though I didn't heed the call to do this until my late thirties. Nothing helps you become a good student of life better than having some written record of what happened. You cannot trust your memory. I started my journals in spiral-bound notebooks, which was better than little scratch pieces of paper torn and put everywhere. I now purchase a nice book from a store, which is more presentable and easier to manage. A journal should be something you don't mind carrying with you where you go. You'll have to carry it to classes you attend, seminars, church sermons, and any other event where a good idea may be lingering that needs to be grabbed and written down. Take time to review your journal periodically. This way you can see growth and progress in your life. It helps to put perspective on things when they are viewed from a distance.

SUREFIRE STRATEGY 17: Become a constant reader. It's important to fill your mind with good things. Jim Rohn said years ago: "I wonder why every house over a quarter million dollars has a library in it?" That should give you a clue. People who earn higher incomes read good books. Readers are leaders and to get to or stay at the top of your game it's important to read.

SUREFIRE STRATEGY 18: Be careful not to believe everything you hear. Discernment—knowing what to believe and what not to believe—is super-important to success and your emotional health. Discernment is a product of having a good relationship with your Creator and knowing right from wrong. Rumors, gossip, and petty talk have no place in a healthy success strategy. Google and the television don't know everything. Just because Google says it doesn't mean it's correct.

CHAPTER 7

PASSION AND PROFESSION

Now ranked number one in the world in the cruiserweight division, I was on the verge of seeing my dream fulfilled. I had grown up in the karate school environment and had set my goals early, and now I was close. As fate would have it, the karate school I had grown up in was on the verge of closing. I had spent my entire childhood and adolescent life there, watching it closely. I had been traveling a lot training and competing, and at this point wasn't training in the local school like I had been at one time.

One day while I was in town I decided to go back to the ole stomping ground for a class. I wanted to get in a good karate class and check things out. I had heard the school was on its' way out and about to close, due to low interest. It was true: the old group of hardcore martial artists who had driven this place for decades had moved, and the current instructor just didn't seem to have the drive needed to make it work and be profitable. Since the school meant so much to me, I decided to speak with the current owner to try to help, maybe give him some insight, but it seemed to do no good.

That same week I decided to speak with the landlord and check the status of the school. I drove up to the local strip center and parked near the front entrance. As I walked into the business I could see the owner of the center through the hallway. The owner was a pretty successful man, building a small heating and air business to good size organization. I walked swiftly to the counter at the front of the lobby.

"How can I help you?" the lady behind the counter asked.

"I'd like to see Mr. Howard, please," I said.

"Hold on and let me see if he's available. What is this about?" she asked.

"Just tell him the karate guy is here to talk about the karate school next door," I answered.

She picked up the telephone and hit a few buttons. I stood at the counter, shifting back and forth. I could hear Mr. Howard on the other end of the phone. The lady told him "the karate guy," was wanting to talk to him. She said a few more unrelated sentences and hung up the phone. She looked up at me with a slight grin and pointed down the hall, saying, "Mr. Howard is in his office right down that hall. He says he has a few minutes."

I nodded and thanked her, then started the walk down the long hallway. I arrived at the office on the right and stood for a moment staring at the name on the door. PRESIDENT, it said in big bold letters under the name.

"Hi Mr. Howard," I said loudly, as I nudged open the door enough to stick my head through.

"Hey son," replied Mr. Howard in a polite tone. "I thought when she said karate guy, she meant the current tenant next door. How's your mom and dad?"

"They're fine, sir. Dad is working a lot and Mom is busy with my little brother."

"Good," Mr. Howard said. "What brings you here today?"

"Well, sir, it's about that karate school next door. I wanted to see what's going on. I've been away a good bit and haven't been able to get over there much."

"Yes, I've been hearing about your matches a lot," said Mr. Howard. "Congratulations! I hear you're one of the best in the world now."

"Yes sir," I answered as humbly as possible. "I've been doing pretty well. Knocked a guy out recently in New Hampshire."

"Yeah, that's what I saw in the paper," Mr. Howard said, smiling. "To be straight about it, I'm about to lock the doors on the karate school. He's gotten six months behind on his rent and I can't let it go on any longer. I've given him every opportunity to do what's right and catch up."

"I didn't know he was that far behind, sir," I answered in amazement sort of looking around the room, like an answer to that problem was going to jump out from somewhere.

"I can't let a tenant keep using me as a free place of business when I don't get any free rent." Mr. Howard smirked.

"Mr. Howard, I understand your position, but I sure do hate to see it close."

"Why don't you take it over?" said Mr. Howard. "You definitely got the knowledge, it appears."

"I … I guess I could look into it," I stammered, "but I'm in college, competing frequently and training all over the place. Not sure I'd be able to make it run like it should being gone as much as I am." I paused for some reason in midsentence, then looked over at Mr. Howard and said, "Could you give me a week before you lock him out, sir?"

"I really don't want to give him another free week in there; he's had plenty of chances. But since your dad has done so much business with me for years and I respect *him* so much, I'll let that guy ride one more week. Next Friday this time, you come in here and maybe you can get him to pay."

"Thanks, Mr. Howard. How much does he owe you right now?" I asked.

"He owes almost two thousand dollars right now and by next week it'll be the first, so he'll owe another rent check."

"Got it, sir. Let me see what I can do and I'll be back next week to let you know."

"Okay, son," answered Mr. Howard. "Please tell your dad I said hello."

I shook hands with the businessman and darted out the door. I now had a week to develop a plan to save the karate school. Not know if this was in the cards or not, I just knew I couldn't let it close without a fight.

I drove home rapidly, my mind racing. What would I do if the karate school I'd grown up in closed? Where would home be? I had been traveling and training all over but there is something special about your first martial arts center. It's almost spiritual, kind of like church. Changing is difficult and not something anyone takes lightheartedly. This was the place where I'd met such good people who loved the art like I did. I met a great first instructor and several young men who became my mentors through the years. Even Eddie, from the very first day I'd walked into the dojo—the gentleman who had complimented me after my first class. Eddie had referred to me as "Hot Shot" as a kid, and now as an adult Eddie worked in a local restaurant I went to often. Eddie had supported me through all these years. He'd come to the dojo and worked out with me as a growing martial artist. He'd gone with me to my kickboxing matches. Even when I didn't do so well, Eddie was there. During the drive home I thought about my life with the dojo and which path to take. All the memories and dreams came flooding back as I neared home.

I pulled my car into the neighborhood where I'd done so many jogs-the familiar neighborhood where me and my buddies had hung out, played games, and had so much fun growing up. I parked beside mom's car and went inside. Dad's truck wasn't home. Dad was out working late.

Mom had been cleaning and the house had a great fresh smell to it. Mom greeted me as she always did, and I went to my room for a bit. I heard dad's truck pull into the drive. Dad drove a dually truck with a diesel engine, so you could hear it way up the street before it arrived. Dad always methodically parked it in the same spot in the driveway so Mom could get out easily without hitting his truck. Dad came in and greeted Mom as usual, then sat down at the kitchen table to open mail and wait on dinner.

I could hear mom and dad speaking about their day's activities and upcoming activities in the near future. I decided to go in and speak with the parents about this dilemma. I closed the desk drawer I'd been fumbling through and went to the kitchen. I sat down at the table next to Dad and began to explain this situation. I explained the current state of the martial arts school I'd grown up in and how the landlord was on the verge of shutting it down. Dad knew where this whole thing was going, but he listened patiently as the story unfolded. Finally, when I wrapped it up, dad looked at me for a moment and said slowly:

"Well son, what do you want to do? I understand you don't want to see it close, but you do have a lot going on right now: school, your kickboxing, and training."

"I know there's a lot here to consider, but I can't stand the thought of seeing it go away," I lamented. "I spent my entire life in that place."

"Yes son, I know, but things change. Starting a business is a big step. It becomes more than just karate when you take over as an owner; it becomes a job. Are you willing to put the time in and make it grow? It's failing now because there aren't enough new students coming in the door. Can you change that?"

"I'm sure I can get it built up enough to stay open. It could be a great way to make a living, you know? What else would I want to do with my life? I wouldn't even need to stay in school then."

"Hold on now," Dad said sternly. "There is no quitting school. You'll stay in school. I know this could work out for you well, but it could as easily not work out well and you'd be stuck looking for a real job with no degree and no work experience. Keep that in mind."

"Okay, Dad, I understand, but I may not need a job, just karate. It's worked in the past."

"Yes, I know, but you'll finish college even if I have to come sit with you every day in class," he insisted. I was the first Hudson to go to college and Dad wasn't going to let me be the first one to start and not finish.

"Yes sir. I don't have the money right now to pay Mr. Howard and get the school back in the good with him, though. Could I borrow it from you? I'll pay you back with the income from the school once I get it back to where it should be."

"Okay," said dad. "You can pay it back on your own terms—just make sure you do right by the students and yourself."

"Thanks, Dad!" I exclaimed, and darted back to my room. My mind racing about the upcoming takeover of the school. I couldn't sleep that night as my mind raced with aspirations of a huge martial arts academy with me at the helm.

Life was going well. Anticipation soared and the deal was sealed. I took over my own martial arts academy at the young age of twenty. Owning my own business at twenty really was a big event for me. In the coming months my training decreased some as I transitioned into the role of business owner, college student, and world-class competitor.

In addition to this new position as owner of the school I still made time to train on my own and with local partners each day. Running the school had become a little more time-consuming than I had first thought. I was answering calls, setting appointments, doing introductory lessons, paying the bills, and doing all the managerial activities that go along with ownership. Each night after a long day of work, school, and teaching class I'd make it a point to stay after and hit the heavy bag for a few rounds. This training kept me sharp both mentally and physically.

One night after finishing teaching and hitting the bag, I headed home as usual. Upon arriving at the house he found a message saying that a gentleman named John Ormsby had called. Ormsby was a kickboxing promoter and manager out eastern North Carolina. He had worked with three other amazing world champions.

I was excited, to say the least. I had been calling trainers and managers all over the country and was really jacked that my efforts were finally starting to get some traction. I was tired of running up a big phone bill without any results. It was close to ten o'clock, but I figured this guy, being a martial-artist type, was probably up late too. I anxiously dialed the number. The phone rang and rang, and finally a man picked up on the other end.

"Hello, this is John," answered the man, who sounded groggy.

"Hello sir. I had a message you had called. How are you?"

John, finally waking up fully, said, "Fine, and who is this?"

I stood in the kitchen, holding the phone, just brimming with excitement. I was so jacked about a potential match or training or something that I failed to identify myself. John rambled on the other end of the line and finally realized he'd never spoken to this person before. Realizing he had just phoned this unidentified person tonight, it clicked who was returning his call.

"I'm sorry," John said, "I must have dozed off or something. I was calling because we are having a special training camp this coming weekend here and I thought you might want to come. There's going to be some real good fighters here."

"When do I need to be there?" I almost shouted, without even asking where or any other details.

"If you'd like to get here Friday night we work out at seven p.m.," John said. Then you can stay the weekend and get a workout in Saturday and Sunday before you leave."

"That'll be great! I'll be there."

So the date was set. The details were taken down over the phone, and John thanked me for calling, even though I'd awakened him from a deep sleep, and said he looked forward to seeing me Friday night. I could barely control his excitement. I knew that if I could spar and be competitive with these fighters, I had a chance to prove myself to John, who had the connections to get me that shot at the title. Honing my craft was important, and to be the best you have to train with the best. John housed one of the top kickboxing training gyms in the eastern part of the country. It didn't matter that it was a six-and-a-half-hour drive away. I was willing to do whatever it took to get that title.

Luckily, at this point in his business career there were no classes on Friday, Saturday, or Sunday, so I could get away and train wherever I felt I'd get the best sparring and experience. One of the young men I'd met at his first karate lesson had reconnected himself with me and became my number one fans. Eddie, my friend from years past, had gone through many life changes and now could focus once again on training and helping me achieve this long time goal.

I finished up the week and Friday rolled around. I packed my bags and put together all my sparring gear. Each time I went to train or compete at a new location there was a ritual I'd use to put together all my gear.

As a fighter you need some important equipment, and forgetting an item usually meant you asked around the gym to borrow something from someone you didn't know, and therefore wear someone else's sweaty gloves or footpads, which wasn't too fun. There are certain things you have to keep private. This crazy ritual started with putting some good motivational music on and laying the big gym bag on the bed.

After packing the bag with everything I felt would be needed I then would go back over the list, starting with my head and going down. I would touch each part of my body and say out loud the name of the piece of equipment it required, while identifying that it was in the bag visually. I'd put both hands on my head and say, "Headgear." I'd look in the bag while holding my head in my hands and see it was there. I'd then point to my mouth with both index fingers and say, "Mouthpiece," while simultaneously looking in the bag to make sure I had two mouthpieces present. The next piece of equipment was my cup. I'd point to where the cup should go and identify it was in the bag. "Shin pads," looking to see they were there. "Footpads, handwraps, gloves, pants." Once I finished the checklist, I'd zip the bag and toss it on the floor.

Once the main bag was done I'd get together my clothes bag with all the needed clothes for the trip. Friday morning about eight a.m. I rolled my vehicle out of the driveway and began the long ride to eastern North Carolina.

The trip was uneventful and the ride was long, but I was determined to make my mark with these high quality sparring partners. My Isuzu Rodeo was packed with sparring gear and a weekend's worth of clothes as I rode north along I-85, through Raleigh, NC, turning right, then heading east toward Greenville, NC, the home of Bemjo Kickboxing and East Carolina University.

My vehicle didn't have cruise control and it was a manual transmission, so driving was definitely an interactive process. I had to stop at a gas station close to Greenville, N.C., to buy a Rand McNally map of where I was going. In this day there weren't cell phones or GPS's and being a young traveler and I was learning my way around the world, my Dad had written step-by-step instructions on how to get to his destination, but once in Greenville I wasn't sure where the gym was.

John had told me on the phone Dickenson Avenue in downtown Greenville, but I had no idea where that was. As I pulled into the town I was busy shifting gears, trying simultaneously to hold a drink, to eat peanuts and to unfold and decipher the map. I turned down street after street looking at numbers on the buildings and glancing back at the map and the piece of paper he'd written the address on. Finally I turned down what appeared to be the road leading to Dickenson Avenue. This particular area of the town wasn't what you'd call upscale. Buildings were old and many had graffiti spray-painted on the boards covering the windows. Some of the artwork was actually pretty good, though, even if it had been done in the dark. I saw names of people plastered on the buildings, and murals of Jesus as well.

I turned right on Dickenson Avenue and there it was: number 199. The famous Bemjo Gym. I pulled to the curb. Slowly getting out of the Rodeo I looked up at the three-story building, questioning whether this was actually the gym I'd heard so much about. The address was correct, and the small wooden sign on the door read "Bemjo Kickboxing."

Excited, I opened my hatch and got out all the sparring gear I'd need. I'd had arrived about thirty minutes prior to workout time, so I hurried as I gathered my things, finally slinging the bag over my shoulder, I locked the car, and opened the door to this world-renowned gym. There were two sets of steps, one going up to the second floor and one going down. A sign on the right-hand side of the wall read "KICKBOXING," and an arrow pointed up. At the top of the steps was a green wooden door with writing painted on it identifying the gym and my anticipated destination for training with champions.

I slowly opened the large green door, which creaked and scraped on the hardwood floor. Down a hallway to the right I could see a canvas heavy bag swinging as if someone had hit it and left it swinging. The round bell was going in the background. Every three minutes I'd hear the loud bell ding, with a thirty-second whistle to alert the trainees that there was half a minute left to get busy and win the round. The familiar smell of gym floated in the air, easing my nerves a bit.

A man saw me open the door and quickly approached. It was John Ormsby, the man who'd called me and arranged this meeting. John greeted me at the door cordially and showed me around briefly. The usual notes: here's the bathroom, here's the training floor. There were a few guys on the floor warming up, shadow boxing, and doing calisthenics. After the brief tour John stopped and asked pointedly: "Are you ready?"

"Yes sir, that's why I drove all this way," I replied.

"Excellent! Go ahead and get your stuff on and Randy will get things rolling here in a bit." John pointed to Randy, who was in the corner wrapping his hands. Randy was kind of eyeballing us two as we did our tour. Taking the cue, Randy trotted over to meet the "new guy" in the gym.

"Randy, this is the number one cruiserweight contender," John said. "He's driven up here to get some work in with us."

Randy looked me up and down, then smiled with a big grin and said, "Good to meet you. I'm Randy."

John explained that Randy was the head trainer there. He was a local college kid who was studying exercise science and sports medicine, with a passion for martial arts and kickboxing. Randy directed me over to a row of chairs to put down my stuff and prepare for the workout that evening.

We both sat down. I unpacked his gear to get prepared for some sparring. Randy made small talk as we wrapped our hands. John walked out of the room. Tonight's workout was going to be just some shadow boxing and sparring. I noticed there were only two guys in the gym that night, not counting me. I asked Randy where the crowd was and Randy replied, "Tonight's probably just gonna be us. Dale is getting ready for a fight and taking the night off. He has a tendency to over-train and needs a night of recovery once in a while."

I acknowledged with a nod and continued to wrap up. I was getting my footgear out of my bag when John appeared. "Tonight let's just let the new guy spar with Brendan three to five rounds and do a little ab work, and we should be good for tonight. Tomorrow Dale and everyone should be back training. Tonight we're just boxing. Getting some extra work with our hands."

The boxer on the floor, who they had been watching shadow box, was Brendan, the runner up to the North

Carolina Golden Gloves two years in a row. He was about 175 pounds and known for his tenacity. He had actually gotten the opportunity to be a sparring partner for Hector Camacho once when Camacho was getting ready for a title defense.

I got my sparring gear on and began to stretch out with Randy. I didn't put my headgear on. I thought tonight I wouldn't wear the headgear since I really didn't like wearing it and it made me fatigue fast, mainly because I wasn't used to it. John looked over at me and said, "Where's your headgear?"

"I didn't figure I'd wear it tonight, since we were just boxing," I replied.

Randy gave the young fighter a strange look and said, "Man, you really should wear that headgear."

Knowing what I know now, it wasn't long until I realized Randy had my best interest at heart.

John concurred: "Yeah, we don't want no head butts or injuries that could have been prevented."

So I went back over to my bag and pulled out my red Ringside headgear. I pulled it on and then began to pull my gloves back on over my hand wraps.

Randy looked over at me once he'd pulled on the headgear and gave me his signature Randy nod. Three rounds of shadow boxing was first, prior to sparring. Brendan finally squared off in the center of the hardwood floor. We both had tennis shoes on, since there would be no kicking. After five rounds of just boxing with the Golden Glove contender, I agreed that wearing the headgear was a good call. Brendan was quick and had an exceptionally good left hook, which usually worked really well over the right hand and shoulder of southpaw fighters. Which was me at the time.

Dale had entered the room during our final two rounds. He watched attentively, as he'd heard of the number-one cruiserweight contender coming this weekend. He also knew Brendan was a good boxer and wanted to see how the new guy measured up.

The final bell rang and Dale came over to congratulate us on a good sparring match. We bumped gloves as a sign of sportsmanship and turned headed toward our bags where all our gear was stored. Randy came over to me and helped take off my headgear. I was pretty fatigued and had trouble steadying my fingers to undo the latch under my chin. Randy pulled the headgear off and said with a big grin, "Glad you took my advice, huh, kid?" I nodded in agreement and I tried to thank him, but with my mouthpiece still in and not able to catch my breath, I just mumbled something inaudible, I knew he didn't understand. Randy held up his fist for a fist bump, we bumped knuckles, and Randy went to get John from the back of the training area.

John had his own apartment in the rear of the martial arts school. He was a certified public accountant by day and worked in the kickboxing world because of his love of fighting and the art. He had run a martial arts school for much of his life, while working on his career. When Dale saw John come out of the back they all gathered together in a loose circle. Dale said to John, "The kid did good tonight. They didn't kick, but he probably needed a little work on his hands anyway."

"That's why I put him with Brendan tonight," John answered. "Hopefully tomorrow he'll get some good kicking in with Ronnie and you guys."

"Yeah, you know he and Ronnie are similar in size and build," Dale said. "I bet they kick the same as well." Dale looked at the young man and patted him on the bottom, while saying to John with a smile, "Where's this new boy gonna sleep tonight, John? He gonna bunk with us?"

At first I was a little taken back by Dale's forwardness and his playful demeanor. I had just met this guy and couldn't tell if he was joking or not. The pat on the bottom made me a little leery, and I wondered for a moment what I'd gotten myself into. I had planned on getting a room somewhere for the weekend and training at the gym.

Randy piped up: "He can stay with us. Big Green is empty tonight." Only the regular guys there knew what Big Green was. Randy was referring to his long green vinyl couch in his apartment living room.

John replied, "Sounds good to me. Big Green will probably be a little better than the dojo floor."

With a smile, we all commenced to migrate down the stairs that led from Dickenson Avenue up to the dojo. We entered the street on the curb and Randy yelled across to me: "Follow me to my apartment. It's just three miles away."

Dale jumped in his little car, Randy jumped into a 1986 Cutlass Supreme, which he lovingly called Sugar Bear, and the caravan of fighters were off to get some rest. I was feeling pretty weary now, after a six-hour drive and an intense sparring session with the Golden Glove boxer. I was looking forward to some rest, wherever it was going to be.

The friendships made along one's path to reach a certain goal are sometimes pivotal steps. Friendships made in the gym, banging it out with your partners, are some of the strongest, similar to that of two men who have seen combat together. There's something amazing about two men getting in the ring and trying to kill each other during their training time, but becoming best friends afterwards. People often have a hard time understanding it, but bonds created under hardship are bonds that stick. Over two and a half decades all of us old training partners are still close, despite living three to five hours away. We still speak frequently and are there for each other if one of needs support.

God's plan is easily viewed after the fact. During certain times in life the foundation is being laid and the steps are being constructed, but in the busyness of life sometimes those steps are not visible. Training with these guys, Randy "Big Nasty" Ballard, Dale "Sunshine" Frye, Ronnie "the Kid" Copeland, Tony Geouge, and a host of other colorful characters would prove invaluable to me, as a rising champion, both in skills shared and friendships made. I would travel back and forth to John's gym many weekends in preparation for upcoming bouts arranged by John and his connections.

"After David had finished talking with Saul, Jonathan became one in spirit with David, he loved him as himself. From that day Saul kept David with him and did not let him return to his father's house. And Jonathan made a covenant with David because he loved him as himself. Jonathan took off the robe he was wearing and gave it to David, along with his tunic, and even his sword, his bow and his belt." (1 Samuel 18:1–4)

SUREFIRE STRATEGY 19: Prosper where you're planted. People in today's society think they should be doing something different. Maybe they should be working in another line of work or they should be married to a different person or doing a different activity. God put you in that position for a reason. You must learn to prosper where you're planted. The conditions in which you currently find yourself are probably about the same as those where you'd like to be. What happens to you happens to everyone. The way you respond to the things that happen to you is what makes you a success or a failure.

SUREFIRE STRATEGY 20: Run your own business. Nothing will teach you more about people, life, and processes more than learning to run your own business. Running your own business is not only a huge opportunity to make a living doing something you enjoy; it's also one of the most complete human growth opportunities there is. As a business owner you learn about both sides of the coin: the employee and the employer. You learn how government intervention plays a role in both sides of that coin. Staying on top of marketing, human resources, management, payroll, expenses, operational procedures, and more keeps you on your toes. Learning to deal with people at a raw level of hiring and firing is conflict resolution training like you'll never experience anywhere else. Running your own business will teach you to be an expeditious but thorough decision maker, which is a characteristic of powerful leaders.

SUREFIRE STRATEGY 21: Write a budget and try to stick with it. In today's world, living paycheck to paycheck is the norm. Money isn't everything but it's pretty close to oxygen. Get that budget on paper and let the family know what it's all about. There are only three things you can do with money. You can spend it, save it, and give it away. No matter what your budget, in order to be prepared you must spend 80 percent of your income, save 10 percent, and give away 10 percent.

SUREFIRE STRATEGY 22: Spend time talking with the elderly. I know a lot of people don't like hanging out with the elderly, but they form the fastest-growing part of our population now, and probably the wisest. When you sit and talk with someone who has lived seventy, eighty, or ninety years you gain a whole new perspective. Someone that old has lived through world wars and economic depressions, and has witnessed the moral decline of our society first hand. There may be mistakes that this elderly person has made that they can share with you, so you don't have to make those same mistakes.

SUREFIRE STRATEGY 23: Study history. The only way we can benefit from the past is by studying it. When studying history we should look for bad things that we don't want to repeat, and find out what led up to the event so we can identify those types of traits if they begin to happen again. History can be studied for victories too. Look back through history and find triumphant times to see what led to them. The great victories were derived through careful planning, preparation, and execution. There's no reason they can't be duplicated multiple times. The only way to prevent catastrophic events is by knowing what led to them, so study history.

CHAPTER 8

PIECES COMING TOGETHER

Training with these newfound training team became natural. The group meshed like a Super Bowl–level team playing their heart out all the time. There was Randy, the leader. Although he was the same age as the rest of us, he was an appointed father figure. His apartment was the sleeping quarters for many nights to five, six, or seven fighters. Of course, Dale "Sunshine" Frye, the World Lightweight Champion at the time, was the "been there, done that" man. Several world champions had come from this gym, but Dale was the only one left still active and fighting on a regular basis. Ronnie "the Kid" Copeland was in the same boat as I was at the time. Ronnie was a smaller heavyweight who had taken a similar path to one I had taken. He grew up doing martial arts and set the goal to be a champion at a young age. We had a similar fighting style, although they had never trained together before meeting at this gym. We both had mediocre hands at the time but could kick like nobody's business.

There were several other well-known fighters who came to this gym regularly because of the high-quality sparring, including a light heavy weight whose last name we made into a verb. Nonetheless, I had found a second home, and hoped a shot at a world title here with this motley crew.

Most weekends I would make the six-hour trip from my hometown to the new gym. I had few enough students at the time that I could just say to each during the week: "No class Saturday." I'd leave on Friday and make the trek. As soon as he arrived, I'd put on my gear and get in the ring, anxious to improve my craft.

Randy would lead the workout and monitor our sparring. John Orsmby would often find himself pulling up a chair on the sideline and observing, often shouting terse instructions: "Hands up," "Kick," "Use that jab." Often between rounds, one of the guys would notice John asleep in the chair. When the bell rang for the next round he'd bobble his head a time or two and wake up. All of us knew he suffered from narcolepsy. It wasn't funny, but we always kind of made fun of "sleepy J," as we called him.

John began to get me matches in some local shows. He even had a promoter in his area looking to put on kickboxing matches. It was a great fit: John had fighters and connections, and the promoter had money and the desire to make more of it.

After I had been training consistently for about a year, and sleeping on an egg crate in Randy's apartment, one day John came in to watch the workout. The gym was packed.

I was a usual now, word spread that the gym in Greenville, NC, had some more top notch sparring going on regularly. It wasn't unusual for fighters to show up from all over to get some rounds in. After the workout that day we all gathered in the hallway on the way out to discuss the plans for after workout. These plans usually involved eating, where to eat, and who got big green that night. We all stood around for a few minutes at the top of the stairs and finally decided we'd had enough. As we started down the stairs, John called me and Randy back.

"The cruiserweight champion has to defend his title soon and you know who he has to fight, don't you?" He smiled as he looked at me and Randy.

Randy and I just stared at him in anticipation. "That's right, gentleman—the number-one contender. If I can get the numbers and travel arrangements worked out with his manager we may just be able to make that happen."

We were hanging on his every word.

John continued, "I'll keep you two posted as to my progress. Just keep training regular in case this thing pans out."

We, of course, eagerly agreed, and said goodbye to John for the night. Randy looked at me and said, "Give me your stuff and I'll see you at the apartment."

I trotted off into the darkness, full of hope that he'd get the title shot I'd so longed for. I finished my weekend with the boys training and smiled the entire six-hour drive back to my home town. I arrived back home with a little more pep in my step this time.

I went about his daily activities dreaming that John would call with a solid offer. I went to college, my part-time job, and then to my own karate school every day. I trained in the middle of that crazy schedule, looking forward to heading back up north to train with the guys the next weekend.

The next week, John finally called. It was good news: John had gotten the word from the champion's handlers. The current champion was a go for our match. He had sat on the belt as long as the sanctioning body would allow. He had a mandatory challenge coming up, and fortunately for me, I was chosen to fight for the championship. October 22 was the day it would all come to a head. I'd finally get my shot at the World Championship.

After getting the word, I immediately began making preparations for this monumental occasion. I'd come a long way. Now I was a business owner, a college student with hopes of graduating in the near future, and I'd met a girl at college who was the perfect one in my eyes. That year was bound to be the grandest.

SUREFIRE STRATEGY 24: Stay pure. Watch what you see. Watch what you think. King David said it best in Psalm 4:23: "Above all else, guard your heart, for everything you do flows from it." The eye is the window to the soul. What you see sometimes doesn't go away as fast as you'd like. Images can stay in your brain for days, months, and even years. Ask someone who's been in a horrific accident or someone who's been in war. Images don't go away. So you have to be careful of what goes through that window. Make it a point to look at good things in order to maintain a file of good images in your brain. This purity is not only mental; it's also physical, which is something I've not addressed here.

SUREFIRE STRATEGY 25: Be careful not to jump on bandwagons. Most of the time the masses are wrong. The great marketing guru Dan Kennedy said, "In business you can be hugely successful just by finding out what the majority of people in your industry are doing and just do the opposite." Just because everyone else is doing it doesn't mean it's the right thing. It's a whole lot harder to get off a bandwagon than it is to get on one, and wheels fall off these things pretty quick.

SUREFIRE STRATEGY 26: Give. In the Bible it says you need to give your time, talents, and finances. A stingy person normally doesn't get very far in life. You also need to remember that no one has ever seen a U-Haul truck at a funeral. Whatever you have here on this planet isn't really yours; it's only loaned to you temporarily. Many times when I've run low on cash I made it a point to give a little more than I really could afford, and it came back many times over. This giving creates a cycle. Why do you think they call money currency? Because it flows like water.

CHAPTER 9

BIG WEIGH-IN

Training camp was on. As a new business owner I had to make sure the business was tended to in my absence. My brother and future wife covered for me while I traveled to any gym I could find and get sparring. My brother covered all the teaching while my future wife would handle administrative items. Eight weeks out from the fight, my training details were laid out by none other than Randy "Big Nasty" Ballard. I would leave the business on Wednesday each week and travel to Greenville, NC, where I'd sleep on Randy's big couch, affectionately called 'Big Green'.

I made the six-hour trip each Wednesday and arrived at the gym just in time for the nightly workout. I would leave the business on Wednesday each week and travel to Greenville, NC, where I'd sleep on Randy's big couch, affectionately called 'Big Green'.

As soon as I arrived at the Bemjo Kickboxing Gym I'd run up those big stairs and throw my gym bag down. Randy would always be there to greet me and John would soon come in to watch us train. As training intensified, I'd rise early at Randy's apartment to go weight train in the morning and then do the normal sparring and high-intensity calisthenics in the evening. Many nights at the gym, new sparring partners would show up to see how they measured up. Some came with a super attitude to help me get ready for the upcoming bout and some came with determination to show me that they should be in my shoes. I really didn't care what their attitude was. I just knew I was getting much-needed experience sparring with all types of fighters.

The bonds between us weekend warriors grew strong. We all worked toward the same goal and had many memorable days in the gym, as well as living together as teammates, even when an adversarial fighter would come in to try to prove his worthiness. Each of us would usually bring him into the fold after a great sparring match. We all respected fighters that could put it all on the line. Attitudes were kept in check either by someone getting kicked in the head or by Randy and Dale, the group leaders, calling a poor attitude out.

Sunday night, after the final workout of the week, I would make the trip back to my hometown to make sure everything was operating well the business, and I'd go to classes at a local college. At this time I was college student, business owner, championship contender, and more. Many nights after training in Greenville, NC, the six-hour drive home was a tough one. Sleepy and tired, I'd would shift positions around in the vehicle to get more comfortable and stay awake. Sometimes my feet would be so sore I couldn't press the accelerator in my car. I'd take turns pushing the pedals with alternate feet, and would stop periodically to stretch my legs and find some relief from a numb bottom and throbbing bones.

Finally the week of the big match arrived. I was looking sharp, my weight was perfect, and my mind was clear. Randy gave me a call to solidify the week's schedule, since that Saturday night was destiny for all involved, the team leader wanted to make sure I was on track.

I had been training Mondays and Tuesdays with Eddie at the karate school, and then on Wednesday morning I'd head to Greenville. This regime had prepared me perfectly for the upcoming twelve-round bout against the current champion.

Wednesday, the week of the big match, was like the previous months: I pulled out around ten a.m. in order to make it by workout time. I arrived as usual in time for the nightly workout. Since it was title-fight week the workout was light. Randy had dictated every step of the physical routine, and as it was the week of the fight he wanted to make sure I ended my training on a high note. Tonight there was no sparring, to avoid getting injured the week of the fight. Friday would be the weigh-ins, with the bout taking place the next day.

Friday morning came. I slept in for a bit, and then prepared for the two-hour drive to the venue. The world title match would take place in a convention center next to a Holiday Inn, so weigh-ins would be in the hotel. Randy and I loaded up Sweet Lovin', Randy's new ride, with all our gear we needed (Sugar Bear had passed of a broken engine). Two hours later we arrived at the site. We walked into the hotel and Randy went to the desk to check in and take care of the particulars.

"Welcome to the Holiday Inn," the young lady behind the counter greeted Randy. He told her the names of the fighters in the group as she looked up our reservations on the computer. She quickly pulled keys and a packet of information out of the bottom drawer near the counter. She then explained where the rooms were and asked if there was anything else we might need.

"No, ma'am," Randy answered. "We are supposed to weigh in for the big match tomorrow here in a little while. Have any of the other fighters checked in yet?"

The lady looked down and began typing on the keyboard hidden under the counter. She looked up after brief pause and said, "Yes sir, Neil Singleton has checked into room four oh-four." She handed a phone to Randy over the counter and said, "Would you like me to connect you?"

"Sure," Randy replied without hesitation. He held the phone to his ear and cocked his weight on one leg. "Hi Neil," he said. "I didn't expect you to answer."

I stood there staring at Randy as he carried on the brief conversation.

"That's fine. We'll see you downstairs here in the lobby in an hour. Thanks." Randy hung up the phone and looked over at me. "Weigh-in in an hour, kid. You're in room three twenty-two and me and Dale are in three thirty-three. Go put all your stuff up and relax for a bit. Don't eat anything or drink anything. You want to be dry at weigh-in."

I just smiled, took the key from Randy's hand, and threw my bags over my shoulder. I walked to the elevator with the group. In one hour my lifelong dream would begin.

Both camps met in the lobby an hour later. The champion, a short cruiserweight—maybe five feet nine inches—was standing next to his trainer. I was trying my best to remain calm and look like a champion. I greeted the current champ in front of the entryway and shook his hand. I was doing my best to appear unshaken, but inside I couldn't get over how big the champ's neck was and how much muscle was packed on that small frame.

We all mingled for a bit, and then the promoter and John came down the hall. John and the promoter greeted the champion's fight camp and made small talk for a bit. Pointing at the men's bathroom down the hall, John said to the champion's manager, "Let's weigh these guys down the hall in that restroom."

Neil's manager agreed, and the two groups headed down the hall. Ten or so people entered the men's bathroom, John leading the way. The bathroom was nice and freshly tiled, in typical Holiday Inn style. It was clean, but not made to hold ten or more people at once. The champion and his manager went in behind John, and I followed behind, as Randy held the door for me.

John put a digital scale on the tile floor and pulled a clipboard from his briefcase. He looked up over his glasses and said, "Number-one contender, you're up."

The decision - World Champ (Oct. 22, 1994)

me, my wife, Shannon, my mom, June, and my two sons

IKF US Title

giving a speech & signing books at a local college

me and Mr. Joe Lewis

Hudson family

earning my Black Belt from Super Foot

sidekick in my first World Title fight

earned my yellow belt (1979)

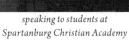

speaking to students at
Spartanburg Christian Academy

I set my bag on the floor and gave my lightweight jacket to Randy to hold. I took off my shoes, shirt, and pants. In my shorts, I stepped up on the scales and took a deep breath. John leaned over the scales, holding on to his glasses as if that would help bring the numbers into focus.

"One hundred eighty-eight pounds for the challenger," he said in a firm, loud tone. I stepped off the scales and Randy gave me the thumbs up and handed me my pants and shirt.

"Now for the champion," John said, looking over at Neil.

The stocky champion took off his jacket and hat and handed them to his manager, then proceeded to take off his pants. He stepped onto the scales and looked to John for the go-ahead. John nodded and looked at the numbers.

"One hundred and eighty-nine pounds for the champion, Neil Singleton," said John in that same official voice.

Neil stepped off the scales, looked directly at me, and said, "I got you." Good fighters are known for playing mind tricks on young challengers. Neil knew his weight was dead on the limit for the cruiserweight class. In his mind, he had an advantage over me by being a pound heavier. Maybe I had missed the mark by a pound. I was trying hard to keep my composure.

Randy nudged me when he saw the mind game taking place and muttered, "Come on, let's get some food."

After going the entire day without any food and very little water or drink, I was ready to scarf it down somewhere. We all proceeded to load up and travel to a small Italian restaurant near the fight venue. Pasta was always a good complex carbohydrate to load up on the night before the big match. Once seated at the table, the fight team ordered, and started to dig in. The food was great, but I couldn't put it away like he had hoped. Anticipation ran through my veins, and eating wasn't a huge priority at that moment. By the same time the next night, I would be World Cruiserweight Champion—I just knew it.

SUREFIRE STRATEGY 27: Read the Bible. I know a lot of people say, "Ah it's an old book that's not really relevant to today." However, if you read the Bible it'll speak to you. Now, your heart has to be open to it and you need to be aware this will happen. The Bible is God's written living word. It's sixty-six books, written by multiple authors over 15 centuries. In those books, God reveals His attributes and His characteristics so we can study them and become more like Him. His Son is talked about all the way through, from Genesis to Revelation.

SUREFIRE STRATEGY 28: Go to church. Nothing revives the spirit and keeps you in check better than good communal worship. We're commanded to get together with other believers and celebrate the love of Christ. Christ came and died for us, so we could live eternally in Heaven with Him. What a plan!

SUREFIRE STRATEGY 29: Don't do drugs. Nancy Reagan had it right years ago when she said, "Just say no!" Life is too scrumptious to mess it up with some chemical that clouds your judgment and thinking. There's enough good out there that we shouldn't need some illegal substance to make us feel good. Your body is a temple and you must guard what goes in it. Being hooked on something you cannot control is no way to go through life.

CHAPTER 10

AND THE NEW

As you can imagine, I was restless the night before the fight. The entire night as I lay in bed, my mind went over all the "what if" scenarios. What if the champ came out real aggressive? What if he came out slow? What if he came out and got right inside looking for an inside fight? What if … what if … it went on all night, until finally the alarm went off for break-fast.

Randy had given the instructions for the team meet in the lobby to hit the breakfast buffet. Since weigh-ins were over, eating was wide open now. On the day of the big match, though—or any match, for that matter— eating light was important. Any fighter will tell you that overstuffing will make you sluggish. After a great buffet, we decided to spend the early afternoon watching a movie. After the movie, we would have a late lunch and nap before it was time to be at the venue for physicals.

Randy and Dale always liked the idea of going to the movies on the day of a big match. The movie was a great way to sit, relax in a cool place, and get your mind focused on something other than that night's fight. Dale had actually just begun a career as an actor, and had been in a few action films. Being a part of that industry seemed to spark a strong interest in what was out at the theater. We all assembled in the lobby and piled in vehicles to head to the movies.

My family was making the trip up that day. My new fiancée, who had never seen a kickboxing match, would definitely come to support me. Of course, Mom, Dad, and my brother would be there too. Eddie, my good friend from way back when I first began this journey, was one of those travelers. Even my Dad's work associates from three states away were making the trip. The six-hour ride couldn't stop all these loyal fans and friends who had followed me since I had started training in 1979. Twenty-three years later, these fans weren't about to miss my title fight. Since I had purchased the karate school it had grown substantially, and many of my students made the trip to see this match. I personally sold over a hundred tickets right from my school for a kickboxing event over six hours away.

We finished our movie and got a light lunch in town. Then we headed back to the hotel for a nap. Though I had hardly slept the night before, I still laid in my bed tossing and turning, playing the "what if" game again. Finally the time came. I was just sitting on the bed staring at my bag with all my equipment when the knock came at the door. It was Randy, ready to take me down to the scene. I opened the door. Randy smiled and stretched out an arm, saying, "Ready, champ? It's time."

I grabbed my bag and walked out into the hallway. Randy was alone and the matches had already started in the arena. Ronnie, Dale, and Eddie were waiting for us in the dressing room. Randy and I walked across the large parking lot and made a stealthy entrance using the side door of the arena, being careful not to get stuck talking to or mingling with any spectators. I kept my eyes down and followed Randy's footsteps toward the dressing room in the back of the arena.

However, my new fiancée intercepted us and gave me a hug. I took off the gold chain I always wore, took out my wallet, and gave them to her to hold during the match. She didn't really say anything as I gave her my belongings. I think she was as nervous as I was. I proceeded to the dressing room.

The team had cleared a space in the back corner of a storage area. This area would be used to get dressed, wrap hands, and do some warming up before I was called out. We usually did some stretches, shadow boxed a little, and did some pad hitting. Fighters always want to get a good sweat going prior to stepping inside the ropes. Going in cold could be a disaster. Randy grabbed two straight chairs and turned them back to back. He sat in one and began pulling out rolls of white gauze and athletic tape to wrap my hands. I sat opposite him and laid my arms over the backs of the chairs, putting my right hand close to Randy's chest. Randy grabbed my hand, gave it a little massage, and began the wrapping process. Every trainer has his own method of wrapping hands. Randy always took into consideration which hand he was wrapping: was it the power hand or the jab hand? Had it been injured in training and was in need of some extra support in a certain area? If so, he'd take special measures to make sure it was addressed. One of the hardest things to do is win a fight when one weapon is not functioning at a hundred percent. Finishing the right hand, Randy looked at me and said, "Make a fist. How's that feel?"

I did as he was told and in a low voice replied, "Feels good."

"Let's see the other one," Randy commanded. So we switched hands and the process began again on the left side. Once this was complete and both hands were prepared for battle, I stood up and grabbed my shin guards and footgear. I had done this hundreds of times, but never with so much adrenaline pulsing through my limbs. I put on one shin guard at a time, taping it at both ends to secure it. Then I slid the boots over the shin guards and taped them together. The tape was added to the boot to secure it as well. Next came my fight pants, and then my black belt. There were many kickboxers who didn't wear a karate belt when they competed, but it was important to me. For a moment, as I fastened the belt, I remembered standing with my Dad in the doorway of the karate school—the school I now owned—and seeing the black belts on the people inside.

Once the gear was ready and I was prepared, I did some seated stretches to loosen my legs. Randy held an air-shield target for me to do a few kicks on. I popped the pad lightly at first, increasing power each time. The matches were going on outside the dressing room and we all could hear the roar of the crowd. When a fighter in the ring took a good shot you could hear the crowd *ooh*ing in astonishment. None of this seemed to bother me or the other guys. We all knew what was happening, and the time was drawing near. Randy put on my favorite black robe, which had my name on the back. He opened the robe, telling me, "Let's put a little Vaseline on your ribs." Randy rubbed the grease on my body. Then, looking into my eyes, he said, "Let me see your face." Dipping out a glob of grease, he rubbed his hands together and smeared it down my nose, over my eyes, and around my cheeks.

Cuts were something you didn't want to have to deal with in a fight, and you prevented them any way you could. Of course, a good defense is the best way, but some blows slip by no matter how good your defense is. That Vaseline would help the leather glove slide off and not catch and tear the skin. Going to the emergency room after a bout is never fun, even if it's a winning bout.

As Randy was finishing up, a young man holding a set of red gloves came through the curtain.

"Hurricane!" he shouted.

Randy held his hand up so the glove runner could see where my team was sequestered. The young man handed the gloves to Randy, saying, "Go get 'em, Hurricane!"

Randy took the gloves and gave one to Ronnie. They began to loosen the laces on each glove, making sure there was enough room to fit the fat, puffy hand wraps. Once they were sufficiently loosened, Randy held the right glove down for me to stick my hand in. Ronnie handed the other glove to Dale. Dale was the most experienced at lacing gloves, and was an expert in a technique called "skinning them back."

This technique comes from way back in the old school days of boxing, when the leather on the glove wasn't as taut and well-made as it is today. Dale took the glove and turned it palm-up. He leaned his body against the glove, with the glove on his abdomen area. He began to tighten the strings, one side at a time. Once each side was as tight as possible, he'd grab both strings and pull them together. He repeated this motion over and over, until the strings were tight all the way to the top of the glove. He then turned over the glove, palm down, still applying pressure with his abdominal area, and tied the first tie—the same knot you'd use tying your shoelaces. He took the beginnings of the bow and pulled the strings down to the finger area of the gloves. The strings were now across the top of the gloves where the fingers curl over to make a fist. Dale then pulled each end of the string to tighten the laces over the back of the glove, pulling the excess, loose leather with it as the strings tightened and ascended toward the wrist. Doing this pulled that leather snug. That snug, tight-fitting leather over a set of ten-ounce boxing gloves helps cut an opponent in the event of a solid blow. Any edge you can get in a twelve-round world championship fight is important. The champion's team was surely skinning his gloves back as well.

Dale completed the right hand, and then did the same with the left. I was ready to enter the arena now. The crowd became antsy as the final preliminary bouts were over and a brief intermission before the main event was wrapping up.

From the doorway leading into the arena the challenger could hear the announcer get the crowd in an uproar when he announced: "And now for the main event!"

As tradition dictates, the challenger was called in first. Before the match, he had gotten to choose which corner he preferred. He chose the blue corner, which meant he wore the blue gloves. I had the red gloves. Once the champion made it to the ring and did a lap or two around the middle to jeer the crowd on, the announcer made the call for the challenger: "And in the red corner, weighing in at an even one hundred and eighty-eight pounds, from Lyman, South Carolina, with a professional record of eighteen wins, one loss, and twelve wins coming by way of knockout. The number one contender in the worrrllld …" The announcer drew that last word out and let it hang for a moment before he said: "… Kevin 'Hurricane' Hudson!"

Randy emerged from the back of the arena with me close behind. Dale was behind me, followed by Ronnie and Eddie. AC/DC's "Hells Bells" began playing. The chiming filled the arena as the lights had been dimmed to build the electric moment. Then the spotlight shone on my black-robe as I stood near the back of the arena. I just rhythmically bounced to stay warm and lose. Then we all began to make our way to the ring. The anticipation was overwhelming. We had worked to prepare for this day and they we were going to see it through.

Randy jogged up the steps to the ring apron and opened the ropes. I stepped through and took an extra hop to clear the ropes, then went on my lap around the ring, waving to the crowd with one hand. The crowd was electric with excitement. Some of my hometown friends had made a huge banner for the event and were holding it up in the back row, shouting "Hurr–i–cane, Hurr–i–cane, Hurr–i–cane!" The champion and I settled into our respective corners for the referee to do his final inspection of us both. The ref would usually start at the boots and feel the feet and shins to make sure they were padded and protected properly. He'd ask if the participant had a cup on, and would then hold up the gloves, looking at the tape job, making sure no laces were exposed that could scratch or get into the eyes of the opponent. Finally he'd say, "Mouthpiece?" pointing to his mouth. Once the fighter acknowledged all was go he'd do the same to the other fighter. This all took a couple of minutes to complete. The entire time the referee was doing his checks the chant was going. The crowd was restless, and most of them were on their feet. The referee then went to the center and called us both in for the final instructions. The champion and I walked to the middle. Neil had his main corner man and Randy walked in behind me.

"Gentlemen, you each have heard the rules. Obey my commands at all times. Keep the kicks up and protect yourselves at all time. Touch 'em up and come out fighting at the bell."

We bumped gloves in the usual sportsmanlike fashion, returning to the corner to get ready for the first bell. I went back to my red corner. Randy, Ronnie, Dale, and Eddie were outside the ropes just on the apron. Randy put my mouthpiece back in and gave me the final hug. I went to each of the four teammates and got that prefight hug. Fighting is serious business and there have been deaths in the ring so hugging your teammates before entering was a tradition we all held dear. Randy began to step down off the apron and yelled: "Let's do it!"

The bell rang for the beginning of round one. As you can imagine, we both came out strong in tit-for-tat exchanges. From the very beginning of the match, I controlled the distance with my superior kicks. Singleton was the stronger fighter and kept pushing the attack, but I managed to constantly kick and move laterally to the side, being careful to stay away from the corners and not get hung up on the ropes.

Rounds two, three, and four consisted of relentless pursuit by the champion and my evasive counter-fighting. In round five things started to slow down a bit. Singleton in his continued advancement got careless and turned forward to throw an overhand right. I shifted my weight to my rear leg and launched a right leg side kick into the champion's midsection. The champion took the brunt of the blow below the sternum and dropped to the floor. The champion landed on his bottom and then jumped right back up as if nothing had happened. The referee did not view this as a knockdown, which was somewhat upsetting to me and my camp. Round five came and went with the fast pace continuing.

When I went to my stool after the sixth round, fatigue had set in. I wondered whether my conditioning was sufficient. Was I really in shape enough to make it? The stress of the event and the magnitude of what was happening weighed heavily on my mind. Randy took my mouthpiece as I sat on the stool. He gave it a little rinse, gave me a sip of water, and said, "You're doing good. That's the end of round six. You're halfway there, baby!" While Randy was giving instructions, Eddie held the ice pack on my neck to help bring my body temperature down. Dale was busy repairing a small cut that had opened up over my right eye. I led as a southpaw most of the time, with my right foot in front, so the right side of my face took most of the punishment that slipped by my defense. The cut wasn't large, and the bleeding hadn't caused much of an issue; Dale just wanted to make sure it didn't get any bigger and risk the referee or doctor stopping the bout.

Rounds seven and eight were clearly mine. I could see the light at the end of the tunnel and now was spurred on by the thought of finally realizing the dream that had been planted inside me as a little boy many years before. Round eight came to a close and I turned toward the red corner to get that one-minute reprieve. I sat down and spit my mouthpiece into Randy's hand. Randy squirted water directly on my face, hoping to bring some more life out of my tired body. Dale worked on the cut and said in my ear: "Kid, this is the home stretch, the final four rounds. You got this thing."

I couldn't speak audibly back at this point; my affirmative communication was simply a nod and a grunt through my rapid breathing. The whistle blew to signal ten seconds until round nine. The referee yelled in a loud voice over the crowd's roar: "Seconds out." Both Neil and I rose to our feet. I wiped the sweat from my brow with my glove and glanced to the front row on the left side of the red corner. A familiar figure sat with his legs crossed and broad smile under a thick beard. He sat calmly while the people around him cheered and yelled. His piercing blue eyes smiled up at me as time seem to stop momentarily just so I would know that there is no such thing as a capricious God.

The referee pointed over at me and shouted, "You ready?" He pointed to the blue corner with the same question. Neil's corner was a little slow getting the stool out of the ring, so the referee gestured to the corner man to move faster. The fighters nodded and stepped out for round nine.

Tired though I was, my conditioning seem to kick in during these last four rounds, determined and preprogrammed by hundreds of rounds of sparring and preparation. My ability to out-move and out-kick the champ hadn't failed. Despite my immense fatigue, I was moving lightly and sticking those kicks wherever I found a hole in the champ's defense.

The final seconds of round eleven came to a close as the bell rang. The timekeeper had to ring the bell multiple times due to the high volume of the crowd's cheering. The referee would glance to the timekeeper to affirm the bell had sounded and break us from what was usually the middle of a flurry. As the referee jumped in between us to mark the end of round eleven we both took a step back and turned toward our respective corners. Neil, in the heat of the event, had to be led by the referee back to his corner. He had gotten turned around in the heat of battle. As I plopped down on the stool, Randy, with excitement in his voice, pulled out my mouthpiece and said, "Time to close the show, baby! Round twelve coming up." His instructions were simple for this last round: Keep doing what had been working really well in the last four rounds. Use those good kicks to keep the champ off-balance and sit down with a good straight left hand when the opportunity arises. Stay off the ropes and don't get caught in the corners.

Eddie held the icepack on my neck, while Dale put a few final touches on the cut that that had opened up several rounds back. The cut had never been a factor. Between rounds Ronnie would mix a paste of Vaseline, adrenaline, and powder and hand it to Dale. Dale would make sure the cut was dry and the paste was applied liberally. The whistle blew to signal the seconds out of the ring. The referee yelled, "Seconds out!" He called us to the center to touch gloves before the beginning of the final round. Fatigued and what felt like slow motion we touched gloves. The referee jumped in between us to give us space and looked toward the timekeeper for the bell to start round twelve.

Once the bell rang, I walked straight forward and threw a hard side kick. Without making contact with ribs or body, it landed on the arms of the champion, knocking him back two steps. I moved laterally to avoid the champ's rebound attack and started pumping that jab and side kick as much as my tired body would allow. My kicks really never let me down. During the entire twelve-round fight I threw as many as twenty-five kicks per round, dropping off to thirteen in the final round. The rules stated that each fighter must throw a minimum of eight kicks per round or risk a point penalization. I had never had that problem throughout my career, and sure wasn't going to have it tonight.

Round twelve was a heated battle, with both of us pouring it on as much as possible. The crowd cheered louder than any round. My family and fans were on their feet. The hammer struck by the timekeeper signaled there were only ten seconds left in the round. The referee broke us, since we had clinched for a second, and shouted, "Ten seconds!" We both went forward and collided in the center of the ring. A heated exchange punctuated the final seconds. The bell rang and the referee had to break us again in mid-stride. The entire crowd was on its feet, and some were standing in chairs to get a better view.

When we realized the fight was over, I'm sure both our reactions were the same, a reaction of relief and agony. Neil walked back toward his corner and draped his arms across the top rope in fatigue, leaning over while his corner man removed his mouthpiece. I thrusted my arms into the air in what I thought was a victory. I wasn't celebrating a win; I was celebrating completing a twelve-round fight with a relentless beast of an opponent. Randy jumped through the ropes to give me a congratulatory hug, followed by the rest of the team. Randy proceeded to direct me back to the red corner while Dale and Eddie removed my gloves. Randy went over to congratulate the blue corner on a well-fought match.

As Dale and Eddie removed the worn gloves, all I could muster was, "Do you think I got it? Do you think I got it?"

Dale and Eddie both nodded, saying, "You got it, champ." But both my team and Neil's team seemed to think enough had been done to wrap it up. We all had a slight bit of concern though, knowing that any time you leave the decision in the judges' hands you run the risk of being on the wrong end of a bad decision. I had suffered that fate early on, and knew that it was a possibility. The champ paced back and forth between the blue and white corners as the judges tallied their scores. I stayed around my corner, with a towel in my hand. Dale followed me around, putting ice on that cut over my eye. It had begun to bleed again during the final round.

Finally the referee went to the score table and spoke to the announcer. The crowd had quieted down some during the tallying of the scores. The referee turned back toward the center of the ring, calling both me and Neil in for the decision. Neil stood on the blue corner side and I on the red corner side. The referee grabbed the inside both my inside hand and the champs by the wrist in anticipation of raising the side that was called the winner. The announcer finally took a deep breath and raised the microphone to his lips.

"Ladies and gentlemen, let's give these two brave warriors a round of applause!" The crowd emitted half a minute of rapturous applause. I was rocking back and forth on my feet, unable to stand still, awaiting the decision.

"Some of the best kickboxing I've ever witnessed," continued the announcer. "And we have a decision. Ladies and gentlemen, judge number one scores the bout one hundred and thirteen to one hundred and ten for the red corner!" The crowd reacted to the announcement, leaving the announcer waiting for enough quiet to complete his next sentence. I had my left wrist trapped by the referee and I held my right fist clenched against my forehead as if encouraging the announcer to go my way with every word.

"Judge number two scores the bout one hundred and thirteen to one hundred and twelve for the…" a pause for drama ensued, then… "the blue corner!" The crowd reacted, but not as strongly. Neil was from the Chicago area and didn't have much support in the crowd, with the exception of a small group of Singleton fans who had made the trip down.

Finally the announcer took a long, deep breath and surveyed the ring, making sure which corner color we were in again. He then pulled the mike again to his lips and said, "And judge number three scored the bout one hundred and fourteen to one hundred and twelve, for the winner …" another one of those pauses came as the crowd grew as quiet as a church mouse, "… and *new* Cruiserweight Champion of the World … Kevin 'Hurricane' Hudson!"

The referee raised my left hand and my right hand automatically went up at the same time, as if they were hooked together. Randy turned and grabbed me by the waist and hoisted me into the air. The crowd went wild, with screams of *"Hurr–i–cane! Hurr–i–cane!"* and my family rushed into the ring to congratulate the me, the newly crowned champion. I had my hands high as Randy toted me around for a moment. As soon as I hit the canvas of the ring, I looked my new bride to be. She had just witnessed her first-ever kickboxing event, and it had been a barnburner. I spotted her in the crowd, making her way to the ring. My little brother made it to the ring before the rest of the family. Being eight years younger, and small, he speedily wiggled his way through the crowd to give me a big hug. He had witness everything I had to go through to finally make it to this level.

My future wife finally made it through the crowd, greeting me with a big smile and a hug. The ring was so full of people that the announcer had to announce over the arena that the ring needed to be cleared. A fear of the ring collapsing was mounting in the promoters, and people's safety was first priority.

People slowly exited the ring, leaving me and my family, along with my team. The announcer glanced in my direction, and I motioned for the microphone. I took the mike and proceeded to thank everyone for coming, and for all the support they'd shown through the years. It was an emotional time for the entire team. Once everything settled down, and all the pictures were snapped, I asked my team where my World Championship Belt was. I remembered having a conversation with the promoter and John. John was expressing his concern in having to pay the champion such a hefty purse to get him to come that he might not be able to swing buying a belt. I had told John I understood that it was a hefty amount of cash but he would fight for the world title for any amount of money as long as the promoter would buy the belt. I had dreamed of that belt for years. The money wasn't as important as having that title and a belt to go along with it.

Randy went to the promoter to inquire about the belt and found out that it hadn't been purchased. He shared the news with me. My future wife consoled me by saying, "You're the champ now, with or without the belt." That satisfied me for the moment. I was happy just being the champion.

In the dressing room, I was seated on a chair behind the arena. People were gathered around the area as I sat to collect myself, with my future bride and family close by. Randy cut my hand wraps from my hands so I could continue to remove tape and gear from my body. I glanced up and saw the former champ and one of his corner men coming through the curtain. Neil approached me and my team with a big smile.

"Congratulations, champ!" he said as he patted me on the shoulder. "You fought a great fight and earned the win."

"Thank you. Thanks for fighting me and giving me this opportunity," I said.

"You're welcome. Can I give you some advice, champ?" Neil said with a big grin.

"Sure," I replied.

"I was the champ for a long time. I knew it couldn't last forever, so enjoy it while you can, and remember people look up to you—especially kids—so stay straight."

I nodded in agreement and smiled while Neil was speaking. I stood up and hugged respectful warrior, saying, "Thanks for your advice. You're a class act and will always be a champ to me."

Neil thanked me and turned to exit. Before he turned, Randy, Dale, and Eddie stuck out their hands to shake Neil's. Neil obliged and said goodbye. Randy grabbed some of the gear to put into the gear bag and told Dale to grab some ice to put on the swelling over my eye.

It had been a long night, and tomorrow I had a six-hour drive with my family and future wife to get back home. But it would be fine, because now I was the World Cruiserweight Kickboxing Champion!

I had finally hit the mark, or so I thought at the time. It's the journey that's more important than the destination. I would realize this as time progressed, but I could mark one goal attained in my life long list of accomplishments to pursue. Remember this, "Trust in the Lord with all your heart, and lean not on your own understanding. Think about him in all your ways and he will make your paths smooth and straight." (Psalm 3:5)

SUREFIRE STRATEGY 30: Get really good at one thing. A child who finds a passion and studies that passion for five years or more is more self-confident, has a higher potential of staying in school, and interacts better with his or her peers. A child who jumps from activity to activity and never finds that one thing that lights their fire generally has lower self-esteem. Being good at something brings pride to a child and instills the thoughts that they do have an inherent worth. Even as an adult, starting late, but finding something admirable that they can be really good at does wonders for their self-image, so get out there and get good at something.

SUREFIRE STRATEGY 31: Teach something. Someone is watching you and learning from you right now. As Zig Ziglar says, "If you're anyone to someone, you're someone." I'm sure you're someone to someone right now, but everyone needs to learn to teach something to someone. Whether you're teaching kids or adults makes no difference. Teaching is a mature activity that requires patience, caring, and great communication. Our world needs great communicators and teachers. In today's society the ability to communicate is diminishing due to text, email, and other forms of person-to-person communication. Being able to take a person from zero knowledge about a subject to average knowledge in a set time period brings pride and self-worth to both teacher and student.

SUREFIRE STRATEGY 32: Have good posture. Try to stand up straight. I know your mom and grandma probably told you all the time: "Pull your shoulders back. Hold your chin up. Have good posture." Having good posture not only helps with chi (energy) flow, it also helps sustain strong bones and healthy muscles. The human body functions better when not slouched. So stand up straight.

CHAPTER 11

STILL NOT SATISFIED

Now that you're familiar with the story of how the Hurricane became the best in the world, let's tell you what happened after that. As Paul Harvey used to say: "And now for the rest of the story." I was just twenty-three when I fulfilled that lifelong dream. Having found my passion early, I set my goals when I was young and began to chip away at them, even if sometimes I didn't know which way I was going. Growing up I knew that fame and fortune lay just around the corner with the accomplishment of this feat, but reality is often harsh. God had a plan, and even though it's taken some twists and turns it's always been where it should be and how it should be.

I won the world championship in 1994, a hugely productive year for me. Not only did I win my coveted world championship; I also graduated college, earned my fourth-degree black belt, moved my business into a new building—where it remains today—and married the girl of my dreams. Years like that don't come around often. A monumental year that would set the wheels in motion for the next chapter of my story.

I won a world title in a sport that was dying out slowly, at least at the professional level. As I was growing up there were kickboxers being televised on ESPN. So I'd watch these guys in awe, many of whom I would spend time with or even train with. About the time I rose to the top of the ranks and achieved my world title, the sport of kickboxing was in a lull. The notoriety had decreased and the possibility of making a living doing it was impossible. So I kept fighting, teaching, and searching for the next big prize.

After winning the championship in '94, I fought whenever there was a match to fight. Due to the lack of organization of the sport there weren't a lot of shows being promoted. Kickboxing was still a huge part of my life; however, I did become somewhat disgruntled as a participant in a dying sport.

I thought I'd turn to boxing. It seemed like a natural transition, and my hands had improved tremendously through the years due to working with good sparring partners and isolating the hands frequently.

Being in the fight community, I was familiar with boxing people as well and hooked up with a manager that seemed to have connections. The chance of getting a good Caucasian boy who could box was exciting to a manager located about an hour away from my home.

I began making a weekly trip down to Columbia to spar. I was a world champion in a sport that didn't bring fame, as I had assumed it would. I figured that with the experience I had it would be a smooth transition.

The gym in Columbia was a racquetball court in a fitness center, with a ring, speed bag, and a few heavy bags hanging around. There was a timer mounted on the wall, which ran all the time. My little brother would cover the school back at home and allow me to get down the road to make a six p.m. workout time. This new manager saw promise in my ability and quickly lined up some "easy" wins for me. The boxing game was unlike the kickboxing world I was used to. In the kickboxing world, it seemed, everyone was pretty much on the up and up, maybe because they mostly came from a martial arts background. In the boxing game, as I soon found out, there were a large number of unethical people just trying to make a dollar off some poor fighter. Managers would pad the record of a fighter who had some marketability up to maybe seven or eight wins with zero losses, then try to pitch him to a bigger promoter on television for some money.

I fought in a few little towns around North Carolina, and got a few of those "easy" wins. I built up a pro boxing record of three wins and zero losses when the manager came to me and said, "Boy, you ready to go big time?" I had made the trip down and just finished sparring ten rounds with a heavyweight who was one of those padded fighters. He had a huge winning record, but his toughest opponent was maybe equivalent to an overweight mad eighth grader. I had done well in the ten rounds and Billy the manager was in there to observe. He normally only frequented the gym when he was trying to set something up.

I looked at Billy through the sweat and headgear and replied, "Yes sir."

"Good!" Billy squealed. He grinned and continued: "Meet me outside in the hall once you get cleaned up."

I proceeded to the locker room for a quick shower. I just hated driving the hour and a half back home all sweaty and stinky. I exited the locker with my bag in hand and saw Billy and a couple of other fighters sitting on a bench in the hallway. They were watching a couple of guys in the ring through the glass in the wall. I sat where I could see the sparring pair. Billy nudged one of the two fighters sitting next to him and said, "Why don't y'all go get Don and see where he wants to eat. I told him I'd take him to eat if he did ten rounds with the Hurricane today."

The two guys did as instructed and Billy turned his attention toward me, the gullible young man next to him. "How'd you like to fight on the Lewis–Golota undercard in two weeks?"

I was never one to turn down a match. "Sounds good to me," I replied. "How many rounds?"

"Just a four rounder," Billy said. "They had a fighter fall out and Don King called me to see if I could get a replacement. I thought about you." This was definitely a big opportunity. To fight on the undercard of the world heavyweight championship at the Trump Arena in Atlantic City was nothing to pass up. At the time, I was only three wins into my boxing career and thought this would be an opportunity to show the boxing world my stuff.

I agreed pretty much immediately, not even asking information about the opponent or purse. I assumed this manager would take care of me like my other team had done throughout my kickboxing matches. The day finally came. I was to meet Billy and one other fighter in downtown Columbia at a restaurant. Billy was planning on driving from Columbia, SC, to Charlotte, NC, to pick up another fighter, and then on to Atlantic City. It would be about a twelve-hour drive. The team of fighters would check into a hotel near the venue, spend the next day getting tests done to clear them with the New Jersey State Athletic Commission, and would fight the next day. We rode in Billy's minivan with all our gear and luggage in the back and on top.

The trip was exhausting. I wasn't able to rest in the van along the way due to Billy playing loud, obscene rap music with the other guys rapping along. It was an amazing ride. How could these guys rest with Master P screaming all the way to Atlantic City? After picking up Benji in Charlotte, we proceeded on north. Benji was a crafty fighter from North Carolina, who had been with Billy for years. He'd actually fought some high-level opponents and had gone the distance with three world champions, but never won the title. He had had over forty professional boxing matches, but had a lackluster record, with around ten wins and thirty or so losses.

At one of the gas stops, I bought a pair of earplugs, hoping to get some relief from this rap party on wheels. I plugged my ears and tried to close his eyes. To no avail. Sleep kept being chased away by a loud bass note or grunt from the speakers. Leaving at around noon put us arriving in Atlantic City around midnight. This would allow us just enough time to get checked in to the room and hopefully get some rest before the barrage of doctors' appointments the next day. I just prayed I didn't room with Billy. He might want to play that crazy rap stuff all night and sabotage my hopes for some much-needed rest.

Finally the motley crew and I arrived in the glittering city on the Jersey shore. I was pretty enamored by the grandiose city, not having visited there until this point. I woke up some as the excitement of fighting on such a big card set in. Even with all my experience, the excitement was always new when the event drew near. We checked into a Holiday Inn within walking distance of the Trump Arena. This was the same arena where the Miss America competition was held every year. We gathered our belongings from the minivan and went to the front desk. Billy took care of the details and divvied up keys. I was slated to room with Benji, and Billy was off with the other fighter to their room. Once in the room, we were so road weary we could barely even hold our eyes open. I plopped down on the bed near the air conditioner and took off my shoes. Shortly after that I was sound asleep with an alarm set for just five hours later. We were both so tired we didn't even know how loud the other's snoring was. Morning would be here soon.

The next morning after breakfast we all went to the first appointment. Billy had the day scheduled so that as soon as we finished with the checkups we could go back to the room for a bit of down time, then off to the weigh-ins at the Atlantic City Casino. The entire day was a day of hurry up and wait. We waited for the neurologist to get a

CAT scan. After that was finished it was off to the lab for blood work, and we ended up, after a brief lunch, at the ophthalmologist. The New Jersey Athletic Commission is super strict on fighters' health and safety, which is a good thing. It helps decrease ring-related injuries and deaths. Many fighters have gotten injured in the past and carried this injury with them to other bouts, which can cause serious health complications.

Finishing up at the ophthalmologist, Billy announced that they would all go back to their rooms for a little rest, and then he'd meet everyone in the lobby for the seven p.m. weigh-in time. I was excited about weighing in on the same stage as Heavyweight World Champion Lennox Lewis. I found out that another kickboxer was fighting the next day as well: Troy was from Texas and had won multiple world championships in kickboxing, and went on to win a world championship in boxing as well. Troy was the first person to do that in history. The casino was decorated in honor of the upcoming fight between the heavyweight champion and Golota. Golota was a Polish fighter who was known for his toughness…and for occasionally being a little dirty in his bouts. He had fought Riddick Bowe three times, with each of those bouts ending in a bizarre fashion due to low blows or illegal head butts.

I sat in the audience where the fighters were assigned to watch these two gargantuan heavyweights get weighed. I managed to sit close to Troy, hoping to get a moment to chat with him about his accomplishments. The excitement in the air was amazing: a heavyweight title fight in Atlantic City was an entire-town event. Finally after all the big guys did their weighing and much of the audience had left, as well as the press, it was the undercards' turn to weigh in. Fighters were called up pair by pair. Not in the order of their bouts the next night, but by their weight classes. The lightest guys weighed first and the heaviest guys weighed last. So me and my opponent were near the end. Being near the end meant staying up to about midnight.

When I was called up with my opponent, the first thing I noticed was how big the guy was. He was a couple of inches taller than me and seemed to have oversized extremities. He had huge hands and feet. I weighed first at 210 pounds. The German opponent stepped up on the scales next, and came in at 222 pounds. We did a couple of poses for the camera and shook hands. We tried to exchange words, but the German boxer spoke very little English. We all made it to bed late that night and slept in the next day as long as possible. The schedule was tight again on fight day. The athletic commission mandated that all fighters be in the arena by three p.m. and couldn't leave once checked in. Bouts were scheduled to start at eight p.m.

I was, of course, one of the earlier bouts. The fighters who were hoping to make a name for themselves were early on in the card; the main event was the heavyweights.

At this point I didn't know anything about my fighter—whether he was predominantly a righty or lefty, his record, age, or anything; I had just taken the fight hoping to knock out an up-and-coming and gain a foothold in this new endeavor.

We arrived on time at the arena and flashed our credentials to get through security checkpoints. Lennox

Lewis was somewhere in the arena, and security made sure no one could get to him unless he initiated the visit. As fight time approached, spectators began to trickle into the large venue. I was scheduled to fight fourth once fights began. My bout wasn't set to be televised. I sat down in a chair in the dressing room to begin preparing. Since I was just boxing, preparation wasn't as time consuming. Many times in training I would drive three or four hours to meet a group to spar, and would jump out of the car, wrap his hands, and go. When you're as flexible as I am, unless you're doing a bunch of kicking, stretching is a minor event prior to workout.

Billy yelled across the dressing room to get some chairs so they could begin wrapping hands. I did as I was told, and sat on one of the back-to-back chairs. Billy sat down with me and began a ritual similar to the one as Randy had done when he helped me with my kickboxing matches. It wasn't as thorough or careful as Randy's wrap, but it would have to suffice, because there were no other options here in Atlantic City. Once the wrapping was complete Billy went to find an athletic commission official. The official had to check the wrap job and make sure it was legal. No tape over the knuckles or any foreign objects taped in the wrap. The official looked over Billy's job and nodded, placing a big black 'X' over the back of my hands and initialing the back of the wraps so if they were cut off and rewrapped everyone would be alerted. Once that was finished I put on my trunks and boxing shoes. It was getting close to show time, so I began to shadow box in the dressing area. There were other fighters in there as well, but they had the red corner separated from the blue corner. As time drew closer, Billy brought in the red pair of gloves to put on for me. The athletic commission official was close behind to watch Billy put on the gloves. The official made sure there wasn't any shady activity going on and that neither fighter "skinned" the gloves back too tight, giving them an advantage.

I was ready and set to go the fight after next. Usually at this point with my kickboxing team, Randy would gather up the other guys—Ronnie, Dale, and Eddie—put everyone's hand in the center, like a baseball team would do, and say a word of prayer. If Dale was with us he'd always pray. Billy wasn't the praying type, though, so I knelt in the corner of the room alone and prayed. I knew anytime you got a guy fixing to give it his best effort to knock your block off, prayer was a necessity. As soon as I emerged from the back room, Billy ran over to me and said, "It's about time. I watched your opponent hit the pads on the other side and he's a righty." At this point it made no difference, but Billy thought it would be good to know going in. A Michael Buffer type—the professional announcer who was known for saying, "Let's get ready to rumble!"—announced me first. Buffer himself didn't come in until the headliners were up. As I made my way to the ring I noticed how few people were in the arena. The real fight fans come to watch all the fights, but from the looks of the attendance at this time there weren't many of those. I heard the announcer yell out the German name of my opponent and hold that last syllable for what seemed to be a full minute.

Both of were now in the large twenty-four by twenty-four foot ring. This ring seemed like a football field. "You could hold a track meet inside these ropes," I muttered to Billy, who was just outside the ropes. The referee called both fighters to the center. The rules were given in the familiar fashion, and both fighters backed into their respective corners. The bell for round one gonged loudly and echoed all over the large building. I came out pretty strong initially, throwing a good series of jabs, followed by the occasional straight left hand. During the entire first round I was the aggressor while the German remained on defense, throwing a stiff pot shot every so often, connecting with about one out of every four thrown. Round one ended pretty even, according the judges' cards. I was a little winded from pushing the issue during that round, but wasn't letting up for the beginning of round two. About halfway through round two, I misjudged and caught a strong straight right hand, which wobbled me somewhat. Managing to stay up and move out, I held on until the bell rang ending round two. The size of the ring was a blessing after taking such a stiff shot. Round three was a good round, but I definitely lost that round on points, just not doing enough to pull out the round. The fourth and final round would be the deciding factor in this bout. Both of us had landed some good shots, but the German may have had a slight edge going into round four. I was back on the prowl in round four. Pushing forward to try to close the gap on the taller fighter, I led with the jab most of the round but occasionally got a little careless and led with a hard overhand left. We got tied up in the center a time or two, forcing the referee to separate us. The mallet hit the wood block two times, to signify the end of round four in ten seconds. Fatigue had set in, but I pushed forward best I could. Carrying my hands lower than I should have, I stepped straight into a southpaw's worst enemy: the straight right hand. It was as hard a blow as the German could muster, dropping me to one knee with blood beginning to drip from my nose. I heard the referee pick up the count at six and gained my bearings enough to stand and steady myself. The referee did his usual questions: "Do you want to continue?" "What city are you in?" Then he grabbed me with a hug and said, "That's enough. You're bleeding too bad."

With the wave of the referee's hand, it was called and over. I was devastated, but sort of relieved in a sense. That big German was no rookie. Now I faced a twelve-hour ride home with Billy and the crew, with the loud music blaring and my broken nose throbbing, which made me miserable. I did get to stay and see the main event, though. Lennox Lewis and Andrew Golota for the World Heavyweight Championship, which ended up being a bummer as well. Lewis knocked Golota out in about thirty seconds, much to the surprise of everyone. On the good side, I was glad I hadn't had to pay to get in to see that one. The all-night drive back to South Carolina was definitely rough. Most of it was with ear plugs in and an ice pack on my nose.

I was so thankful to be home. My new wife was astonished at the swelling of my nose and saddened from the evidence of the hard shots I had took.

My next few weeks were filled with doctor's appointments and waiting rooms. I found out my injuries were more than just a broken nose from the German boxer. I had had an old injury that happened during training a year or more ago, which I had been unaware of. This was an orbital fracture under my right eye. The surgery required to fix me up and get me back into fighting shape would be a little more extensive than I'd anticipated, and a lot more painful—close to a broken jaw, but not quite that bad.

After the surgery I went home with a saline-filled balloon in the sinus cavity under my right eye and a tube running out my nose. This attractive piece was worn for six weeks while the trapdoor fracture, as they called it, healed. The combination of this thing in my face with the splints in my nose and the inability to breath made for a long six weeks. During my recovery, my brother and some other black belts covered the classes at the dojo. My recovery was slow, but my drive to succeed wasn't hampered.

During my recovery, through some research and friendly conversations with those in the boxing business, I found out some interesting things about my manager, Billy. Billy was notorious for fixing fights, padding fighters' records, and not being truthful with his signed fighters. For instance, I discovered that the match I had just competed in Atlantic City actually paid a lot more than I had brought home. I also found out that the opponent I had faced wasn't just an undefeated boxer like I was at three wins and no losses. The German was a celebrated Olympian, with over three hundred amateur wins. I had trusted Billy to take care of me, but it appeared that Billy only took care of himself. It all made sense to me now. In the previous fight Billy had arranged for me, I was supposed to fight a guy who had four wins and one loss. No one ever mentioned to me that this guy was also the son of a former world champion with an extensive amateur career. Despite my experience in kickboxing, once an opponent gets inside kicking range it can become difficult for a kickboxer to adjust. Many boxers that I would face had fought in as many as two hundred amateur bouts. So their ability to work with just two weapons was superior to a man who'd worked with four weapons pretty much his entire life.

I had been caught up in what I thought I should have been doing and not listening to wise counsel. The answers to questions that should have been asked before going into this deal were now being answered late in the game, wasting the talent that could have been brought along slowly and improved gradually. Instead, Billy threw me to the dogs for a quick buck, not caring about me or my wellbeing either physically or financially.

I had hastily jumped into a deal that brought me more pain than glory. After several stitches, a broken nose, and a broken orbital bone I realized too late that a boxing career handled this way goes nowhere fast. I had missed the mark again. My boxing skills had gotten better but the improvement gained in this deal fell short in comparison to the expense and physical pain that was endured.

> [2] For gaining wisdom and instruction; for understanding words of insight;
> [3] for receiving instruction in prudent behavior, doing what is right and just and fair;
> [4] for giving prudence to those who are simple,

knowledge and discretion to the young—
⁵let the wise listen and add to their learning,
   and let the discerning get guidance—
⁶for understanding proverbs and parables,
   the sayings and riddles of the wise.
⁷The fear of the LORD is the beginning of
   knowledge, but fools despise wisdom and
   instruction. (Proverbs 1:2–7)

SUREFIRE STRATEGY 33: Be slow to sign your name to official documents. Your signature is your seal. In ancient times David sent a messenger with his seal to order the murder of Uriah. I know that, in the business world, signing a note as a guarantor on a loan can hook you in for twenty or thirty years. I know the great Jim Rohn speaks about a time he signed a "continuing guarantee" for a company. They went bankrupt and came to Rohn for the quarter million dollars. He said he finally learned what the word "continuing" means.

SUREFIRE STRATEGY 34: Look people in the eye. When you're talking to people, be interested enough to look into their eyes. This helps in seeing where the person is mentally and spiritually. When I kickboxed or sparred, I always looked the person in the chest, because that way I could see their hips and shoulders. I could see what was coming. The only time I looked my opponent in the eyes was to see where the person was. You can tell if a man's out of gas or if he's got plenty to burn. Many times you can see if a person is ready to lie down on you if you see their eyes.

SUREFIRE STRATEGY 35: Say "yes ma'am" and "no ma'am," "yes sir" and "no sir." Do this to adults as well as children, and teach children to do this. The impression left on an adult's mind when a child responds with a good "yes sir" or "yes ma'am" is amazing. Teachers take kids more seriously when they use this respectful tone. A kid that answers with a "yeah" or "uh-huh" isn't going to do as well in school or life. A good "yes sir" with eye contact goes far. Look at our armed forces. How do they require beginning recruits to respond? It isn't "uh-huh."

CHAPTER 12

TWO TIME

A s the recovery progressed, my business prospered and became a profitable organization. I was married now and spent my time between the growing karate school and my new wife at home. Luckily, we lived only two miles from the business so the commute was brief—sometimes too brief. I could pretty easily shoot up to the school if I'd forgotten something, and once I was in the business alone, I managed to always find something that could turn a five-minute run into an hour. Nonetheless, my new wife was super-supportive and things were moving along well.

Once I was healed up one hundred percent I trained frequently, but not as fervently as I once had. Then one day the kickboxing world called again with a great opportunity. Little did I know when I got the call that this match would radically change my martial-arts path—and my life.

I was called on for a world heavyweight title shot under a smaller emerging kickboxing organization. The bout was to happen in the huge New Haven Coliseum in

Connecticut. In fact, the night before this kickboxing event happened in the coliseum, a music super-group had played and packed the seats. The night of the kickboxing event, however, there were just a thousand or so people in the ten-thousand-seat arena.

I took this opportunity and had the team back in action for the first time since my boxing stint. my training wasn't as stringent as it had been for my first world championship. Life had begun to get in the way of training somewhat. I was now a business owner and husband. I knew the consequences of being lazy on training, though, and if there's one thing that stinks, it's losing. So the regimen proceeded until the scheduled day of departure. I loaded my stuff, and was to meet my team at the Charlotte Douglas Airport in North Carolina for a connecting flight to Connecticut.

I deplaned my first leg on time in Charlotte and proceeded to the next gate, where my team was to meet along with some others who were to be on the card. I sat down at the gate with my carry-on bag and took out a book to read. As I was skimming through the pages, I glanced up and saw a familiar walk. It was Randy coming down the concourse with the others. Beside Randy was none other than Joe Lewis, the first world heavyweight kickboxing and karate champion. I had read about Joe in magazines and books growing up, and was astonished when I saw him. Joe was largely responsible for bringing karate to this country. He had trained with Bruce Lee, and had won more accolades in the fighting community than anyone else. He had even spoken to Elvis Presley on the phone! Randy spotted me seated near the window and walked my direction. I jumped up to greet everyone and make introductions to those I didn't know. This was all done quickly due to our connecting flight boarding while we greeted. We quickly boarded the plane and headed to Connecticut.

I was excited to spend time with a legend like Joe Lewis. Joe turned out to be a hoot to be around, and as down to earth as anyone. He was a walking encyclopedia when it came to martial arts and quite possibly the most knowledgeable martial artist in history. I could listen to him for hours.

Once the plane touched down in New Haven, we all were in for several days of New Haven hospitality. The host of the event was a Catholic priest who was quite an eccentric character. Upon visiting his home near his church, we were delighted to find the father had a long hallway full of autographed photos everyone from John Wayne to Fidel Castro. This guy was amazing—he had actually spent time with everyone he had autographed pictures of. Fidel Castro would mail the father Cuban cigars. We had quite a time eating and hanging out with the father. The day before the event the father treated the kickboxing team to a cruise down the Rhode Island River on a yacht of one of the church members. The conversation between Joe Lewis and the priest was pretty riveting. When you throw in a couple of country boys from North and South Carolina, along with one West Virginian, you know there are some interesting concepts churning.

The day of the event finally came. Randy and I roomed together for this event. The night before the fight was the weigh-ins, as usual, and I initially was three pounds over. I was told I had an hour to sweat those three pounds off. Back to the hotel room we went, where Randy cranked the heat up in the room while I sported my thickest sweatshirt and pants and shadow boxed between the beds. For that hour, I alternated between shadow boxing, jumping jacks, and other calisthenics to sweat out those three pounds. At the second weigh-in, I was right on the dot: 195 pounds. The coach of my opponent was right there watching to make sure I wasn't over—not one ounce.

The opponent for this bout was an Italian guy from the New York area. He evidently hadn't been in the US long, because his English skills were minimal. I waited and prepared in my dressing room while the other bouts proceeded that night. Being the main event was really special but it did have its downsides. One of those was that you didn't get to see any of the preliminary bouts. This night Joe Lewis was the guest of honor and scheduled to do an exhibition with one of his students, which I wanted to see. The student who did the exhibition, John Maynard, later became a good friend of mine and is quite possibly the deadliest man in America. Maynard is one of only three people to have earned a black belt under Joe Lewis, Chuck Norris, and Bill Wallace—a pretty amazing feat.

Randy walked around the brick corner in the locker room, calling for me. As soon as he made eye contact with me, he shouted, "And two-time world champion… You ready, champ?" I had been sitting in a chair smack in the middle of the locker room.

"I'm ready," I replied.

"Where's your mouthpiece?" Randy queried as he looked through our gym bags lying on the floor. Randy took the red gloves under his arm and laid one on the chair and held out the other for me to slip my hand in. Once my hand was in as far as it would go, Randy turned it over and began to skin it back, just as Dale had done so many times before. Dale, Ronnie, and Eddie couldn't make this trip, so Randy and Maynard were cornering for me. Randy finished skinning back the second red glove and grabbed a set of focus pads lying in their gym bag. Holding them up, he said, "Give me a one...Give me a one." I responded, popping out a strong jab at each command. Randy then added a punch or two as I began to break a sweat, and intermittently would stop to shake it out at Randy's command. Maynard came around the corner and yelled, "They're ready!" Randy looked at me and said, "It's time, kid...put ya hands in here." We put our hands in together and Randy led a short prayer for safety and victory.

The announcer made the call and Randy led me into the huge arena as the sparse crowd cheered. This crowd was divided, since the opponent was from neighboring New York and I was a Southern boy. I jumped through the ropes as Randy held them open with his knee and foot. The rest of the corner men stood by the ring with buckets and supplies. Randy jumped in behind me to help him take off my custom black robe that he always wore. He pulled the robe off, gave me a sip of water from a bottle, and put my mouthpiece in when the referee called, "Fighters to the center."

Randy led me to the middle to face my opponent, who was about an inch shorter than me but a little bit broader in the shoulders. The referee gave the instructions that we each had probably heard a thousand times. The referee patted us on the shoulders and said, "Touch 'em up and come out fighting at the bell."

With that, the Italian and I bumped gloves and headed back to our respective corners. Once in the corner, Randy looked me in the eyes and said, "This is it! Two-time world champion! Keep those hands up and look sharp!"

Randy exited the ring to his post down below, and I turned to face the opponent who stood directly across the ring. He was warmed up well, with sweat dripping from his body as I readied myself for the opening bell.

"Ding, ding!" The bell sounded, and as it echoed throughout the arena both of us locked eyes and charged forward. The Italian struck first with a barrage of straight and looping punches, not allowing me to get off my normal attention-getting kick. The Italian fighter muscled me back to the ropes. He pushed me hard, and then made a horrible mistake as I bounced off the ropes. He dropped his guard, not thinking of an incoming blow. He was only focusing on hitting me. I quickly shot a vicious straight left hand down the pipe and connected solidly on the Italian's chin. The Italian crumpled to the ring floor. The referee abruptly sent me to the neutral corner and started the count on the fallen fighter.

The Italian wasn't giving up that easily, though, to my disappointment. He stood and told the referee he was ready to continue. The referee stepped back and motioned the fighters back together. The Italian relentlessly continued to go forward. I was able to sidestep an incoming attack and launch my patented round kick to the head of the aggressor. Catching the Italian warrior around the forehead area, he dropped him to the canvas for a second time. Feeling confident I could end this early and go home a two-time champion, I glanced over to my corner during the referee's count. I could see Randy peering under the bottom rope saying loudly, "Fifteen seconds left in the round! Put the pressure on him."

"*Ding, ding!*" The bell sounded, ending the one-sided first round. Both of us turned from one another to head to our corners for some instruction. I sat on my stool, feeling pretty good about the first round. I had knocked my opponent down twice and won that round decisively. It looked like I was superbly over-skilled for this match, and Randy's instructions were to remain conservatively aggressive, with hands high, and to stay busy. The hammer sounded, signaling seconds out. Round two was starting in ten seconds. I stood with mouthpiece in and hands raised.

The bell rang, and we both moved forward. The second round started out as a carbon copy of round one, with me confidently defending the Italian's punches and moving laterally. Then, for some unknown reason, I zigged when I should have zagged. I stepped straight into a hard right hand. Later, after the match on the way back to the hotel, Maynard stated his admiration for me getting up after that shot. He said, "Hurricane, you couldn't have been hit any harder if you were tied in a chair with your hands behind your back. That's amazing, dude!" I hit the mat so hard after the right hand that my mouthpiece fell out and hit the mat about two feet from me. I landed on my back, and later recalled the first thing I heard after hitting the mat was the referee counting. The referee was on number four when my brain began working again. I managed to roll over onto my belly and began to attempt a pushup. I somehow got to my knees. I looked over to my red corner and saw Maynard picking up the bucket. He appeared to be packing up and leaving. Randy was staring intently at me with his mouth hanging open in amazement.

I felt around blindly, until I found my mouthpiece and managed to grab it with my right glove and put it back in my mouth. Randy saw this and immediately began slapping Maynard on the back saying, "He's getting up! He's getting up!" I stepped up on one knee as the referee reached six, then mustered enough balance to get to both feet as referee hit the number eight. The referee looked deep into my eyes and said, "Do you want to continue?" as he brushed my red gloves on his own shirt to wipe any debris from the ends of the gloves. I answered affirmatively. Then the referee instructed me to walk to him, as a test of my mental stability. I did as instructed, and somehow managed to walk straight and steadily enough to convince the referee I could continue. The referee then looked back at the neutral corner where the Italian fighter had prematurely started some sort of victory dance, and said, "Are you ready?"

The fighter acknowledged, and then the referee screamed, *"Fight!"*

The remainder of round two was pretty much a defensive round for me after that knockdown, which for some reason left no visible marks on his face, and I wasn't even sore the next day. Not sure my brain was unscathed but on the outside, I looked fine. The bell finally sounded as we both were tied up on the ropes near the red corner. I was able to sit directly down on his stool once the bell dinged.

Randy went to work quickly trying to bring some life back to my game. He put ice on my head and neck area. He poured a little ice water down the front of my pants to bring some alertness back into my eyes. "You gotta keep those hands high, and don't step toward his right. Step to the left!" He shouted over the roar of the crowd. The crowd had gotten behind a little more now with my display of true heart and not staying down. Surely several of them were ready to go to the house after they'd seen that vicious knockdown.

This eight-round bout would go to the scorecards for sure. After the Italian fighter had taken such a beating in the first round he'd managed to come back to return the favor in the second round. The bout would end with a majority decision. In this case one fighter was super-fatigued and the other was probably just about as fatigued, which made for a lot of haymakers and a none-too-technical fight. The judges scored this fight in my favor. Officially, one judge had me winning by one point, the second judge had me winning by two points, and the third judge called it a draw. I now was a two-time world champion—it was official!

After the event was wrapped up and I had the belt, the team had to go to the hospital to check on a fighter who had gotten hurt. During the ride over, the team couldn't quit talking about how I had gotten off the mat in round two to win that fight. How no normal person would have been able to recover from a blow such as the one I'd taken that evening. Maynard was going on and on, and finally nudged Joe Lewis, who was sitting in the front seat of the van. "Hurricane did good, didn't he, Joe?" Maynard said. "Tell him what you told me in the locker room. Tell him." Joe, under his breath, muttered three words that he very rarely ever said to anyone: "He did good!"

I had now accomplished my goal not once, but twice, and had met a teacher who would play a role in teaching me so much about martial arts and about life. I wasn't as prepared for this bout as I should have been, but my grit and skill allowed me to pull off a victory. I would train frequently with Joe until his death from brain cancer in 2012. I was blessed to be able to work with one of the greatest martial artists in history. Not only did Joe show me how to fight, he also showed me how to be a man. On his deathbed at the VA clinic in Philadelphia, Joe called in one of his long-time students, who was also a pastor, for some counsel. Joe wanted to be sure he went to Heaven. His student led him down the Roman Road, and Joe was saved just days from seeing the Lord face to face. As tough and hard as Joe lived, he knew that in the end you only had two choices: either live with Jesus for eternity, or not. Joe picked the option that will allow us all to see him again one day, as long as we have chosen Jesus as our Lord and Savior. God bless Joe Lewis.

"Have I not commanded you? Be strong and courageous. Do not be terrified; do not be discouraged, for the LORD your God will be with you wherever you go." (Joshua 1:9)

SUREFIRE STRATEGY 36: Don't use up all of your best resources in the first round. Tougher times are sure to follow. Some fighters are gifted with a strong chin and can take a good punch, but as my buddy Dale Frye says, "You don't want to use all that up." For over six thousand years winter has always come after summer; it happens the same way every year. You'll go through seasons in your life where things are going super and everything you touch seems to work out great. Then you'll go through those times when everything you touch falls apart. Winters come in life. It's best to prepare for them when you can, whether they are financial winters, spiritual winters, or relationship winters. They will come. Don't let the bad times blindside you. Taking a good straight right hand on the chin is better than never seeing it coming.

SUREFIRE STRATEGY 37: Enjoy the journey. Being the best usually isn't as enjoyable as becoming the best. Enjoy the ride and make the best of the ups and the downs. What you become during the journey to achieve a certain goal is what makes life as beautiful as it is. The skills you acquire on the way to financial freedom, to becoming a scratch golfer, to writing your own book, or anything worth accomplishing will help you become the person you desire to be. In *Leadership Is an Art*, Max DePree writes: "We cannot become what we need to be by remaining what we are."

CHAPTER 13

TEAM MEMBER DOWN

Life was going well now. My brother and I were working the karate business. Students were coming in and classes were full. My new wife was working and we were happy newlyweds. Then one night, while I was teaching a kick box fitness class, I was interrupted by his mom, who had begun working with me and my brother at the business.

His mom ran out on the floor with a phone in her hand to grab me. As soon as I saw her approaching, I knew it wasn't going to be a pleasant phone call. She had a scared and astonished look on her face.

She got close to me and said, "Someone's on the phone and wants to speak with you. I couldn't really understand what she was saying, but it was something about Eddie."

I took the phone and held it to my ear. On the other end of the line was a hysterical lady. She said in a sobbing tone, "He went for a run and had a heart attack. They took him to the hospital, but he didn't make it."

"Who is this?" I asked.

"Sharon, Eddie's neighbor."

"You're saying Eddie went out for a run and never came back home, and he's passed?"

"Yes, yes. His daughter and son just came back from the hospital and gave me the news."

I was in total shock. That afternoon, Eddie and I were supposed to eat lunch together. Two hours before our scheduled lunch time, Eddie had called and said we'd would have to eat the next day. He had an emergency meeting at work and couldn't get out of it. Thoughts raced through my head of the times I'd spent with Eddie. The first time I walked into the karate school as an eight-year-old kid. The many runs down Highway 29 with Eddie late at night, preparing for the next fight. The many trips to kickboxing matches. Eating at the restaurant Eddie worked at part-time at while I was going to college.

None of that would ever happen again. My training partner, fellow black belt, friend, and corner man was now gone—just like that.

Eddie's funeral was extremely sad. His son and daughter were in the front row, with his daughter sobbing uncontrollably. Me and several other black belts were pallbearers at the funeral, and carried Eddie's coffin to its final resting place. Any time you lose a friend a piece of you is taken. The only consolation at this funeral was that the pastor who preached spoke of how in the recent months, Eddie had been frequenting his church, and how he had given his heart to the Lord. God had been calling Eddie his entire life, but thank God Eddie didn't wait till it was too late to heed the call.

Eddie passed in 2001, one year after I had my first child. Kickboxing had been sort of slow since winning my second world championship. The next year a call came into the karate school looking for willing combatant again. It was a promoter in Georgia looking to put on a big kickboxing event, and he needed a main event. This fight was to be for the United States Heavyweight Championship, which was vacant at the time.

When I arrived at the school the next day, I got the message and returned the call to the promoter. I was excited to get the call, but wasn't sure whether I should take the fight or not: I had an almost two-year-old daughter at home now, and running the business had become a more and more time-consuming affair. I finally made the decision after consulting with my wife, brother, and Randy. I would fight for the title, and dedicate this bout to my fallen friend and training partner, Eddie.

The regimented routine of training for a fight was old hat to me and I fell right back into it. My new wife understood the long hours and the being away, but she was a little fearful of my chances of getting injured. The orbital fracture had made her more leery of combat sports. My little brother had graduated college now and could help with the business activities even more. My brother had begun fighting in the amateur kickboxing circuit by this time and had racked up a good number of wins as we trained together. The promoter even asked if my brother would fight on the card as an amateur to open the show. What a great event—brothers fighting on the same card! Later on, little brother would win a world championship kickboxing title as well, becoming one of few brothers to win a world championship in the same sport.

For this bout I could weigh 210 pounds, and I wanted to be right on the mark when I weighed in the day before the fight. I remembered how Neil in my first cruiserweight title fight had attempted to gain a psychological advantage at the weigh-ins, saying, "I got you" when I was one pound under the weight limit.

Six weeks of hard training went by fast. Everything was looking good. In the last week of hard training, my brother and I had traveled to Randy's house about three hours away to stay for a few days and complete the finishing touches on our plan for victory. This week wasn't as wonderful as the we all had thought it would be. On the last two days of training I caught a stomach bug and the night before my final day of sparring I spent much of my time in the bathroom. I didn't want to break the rhythm of the training that had been going so well, so I didn't tell anyone. The next morning everyone was up early to get one last training session in before my brother and I had to make the three-hour trip back home.

Randy had fixed a light breakfast for the fighters: a toasted bagel and a balance bar. I could barely get down my juice and didn't eat any of my food. The final day of training was going to be in Randy's garage. His garage had a heavy bag and some fight memorabilia on the wall, and a round timer. It was perfect. Randy announced the plan after everyone had eaten: "Today, boys, we're just going to box and do body rounds." This was just what I needed to hear after spending most of the previous night in the potty.

I wanted to hear we were going to do ten body rounds, with a fresh man in every round trying to hit me in the stomach and rib area.

Somehow I made it through the ten hard rounds with Randy, Ronnie, Dale, and my brother trying to beat me in the belly. I didn't tell anyone what was going on but they had a pretty good idea, due to the foul odors that kept emerging from Randy's garage. Two times that morning, I threw up. I'd finish the round, get my mouthpiece washed out between rounds, swish around some water in my mouth to wash out the bad taste, and the bell would ring again for the next round. Not a pretty picture, but who said being a champion was easy. What a tough ten rounds that was. By the end of the tenth, the whole team knew something was badly wrong with my belly. After the workout and a quick shower, brother had to drive home with me doubled over in the passenger seat with stomach cramps.

One week later, my brother and I piled into the car and made the three-hour trip down to the fight site in Augusta, Georgia. I had recovered pretty well from my stomach bug, but was still weak and had lost about eight pounds due to the sickness. I wasn't going to let this stop me though. I had dedicated this bout to my friend and wasn't going to let a silly sickness get in the way. The prefight interviews and weigh-ins went well, and as me and my brother discussed on the way down to Augusta, I was 202 pounds at weigh in, eight pounds under the limit. My opponent, a muscle-bound natural heavyweight from Atlanta, was right on the money at 210 pounds. During the radio interview he vowed to walk right through my kicks and knock me out. At this point in my career, mind games didn't work. I'd been through a lot and was super-focused on winning, despite the challenging previous week. This was a ten-round bout, and I really hoped I could take this guy out early because I knew, with the week I had had, the further it went the harder it would be.

The team was assembled in full this time. Randy, Ronnie, Dale, and my little brother Shannon were there. Shannon had fought earlier that night and won a unanimous decision in three rounds. Eddie was surely looking down with a proud grin. Randy and the team had gotten me ready in the back. We went through the usual ritual, ending with putting our hands together in a circle, like a baseball team. Dale led a prayer for safety and victory. Many friends and students had made the trip for this momentous occasion. I was the main event. The announcer made the familiar call for my opponent first. Since I was a two-time world champion, I'd get to come in last and make the antsy opponent wait in the ring. Then the announcer called: "In the red corner, weighing in at two hundred two pounds…Kevin 'Hurricane' Hudson!" As soon as the announcements were over, Randy said, "Let's go!" We all jogged toward the red corner. Randy led, with me next, and Dale, Ronnie, and Shannon behind. Randy climbed the steps and held the ropes with that familiar knee-and-foot method. I bounced in and did a lap around the ring with my black robe flowing and red gloves jabbing.

Once the referee gave the instructions in the center of the ring, both me and my opponent readied ourselves for round one. Randy placed my mouthpiece in and I went around to each team member to get the ceremonial hug. "Are you ready?" the referee shouted as he looked toward me standing in the red corner. Then he looked toward the blue corner, where the muscular opponent was, and said the same thing. And then the bell rang: *"Ding, ding!"*

We both moved toward the center, but the muscular opponent seemed to be trying to make good on his promise. He met me about three feet from the red corner and began throwing a barrage of punches. I defended best I could, and managed to slide out to the side and pump that lead jab into my attacker's face. The entire first round was marked by the muscular attacker pushing forward and me, being the smaller of the two of us, moving backwards while punching and kicking. Punching and kicking while moving backwards is an art and takes a great amount of energy. Under normal circumstances, this would have been easy for me, but coming off that virus and being a little dehydrated weighed heavy on my conditioning.

Round two was similar, and the muscular attacker seemed to show no signs of slowing. Ie had won round one on points, but my gas tank was starting to empty fast. A small reprieve from the onslaught came about midway through round two. The muscular aggressor pushed me back to the ropes. I stepped sideways, planted my fight foot and threw a straight right hand, which made contact directly on the attacker's chin. I saw the big man hit the mat and backed up to the neutral corner in order for the referee to begin the count. As I leaned against the white corner post I couldn't help but wish this could be it. I glanced over to my corner while the ref was counting and saw Randy and Dale motioning me to stay at a good pace and not to get crazy with my attack in hopes of taking this guy out. To my disappointment, when the referee reached the number eight, the muscular tough guy was up and nodding his head in agreement to continue.

Knowing I had won that round by two points, I chose to follow my corner's advice and take it easy for the remainder of round two. Trying to conserve energy was a top priority as the fight dragged on into the late rounds.

Rounds three through eight were identical: the big attacker trying to overpower me and my slick movement. Occasionally the strong man would slip one by my defense and the crowd would react. The attacker's corner kept screaming to push the issue, and this guy knew no other route. His kicks were none to pretty as his kicking arsenal was limited to a front kick and a round kick. The round kick never went much above my belt line. By the eighth round, my hips were feeling quite a bit of wear from taking those shin bones over and over. The strong guy's plan may have been to stop the movement that was giving him so many problems—maybe that was the reasoning behind the hip kicks.

Round nine came, and I never really got a second wind. But my will to win this one for Eddie kept pushing me forward. When the final bell rang, I felt confident that I had bagged another title for my fallen friend. The muscle man who had pushed so hard to knock me out had been unsuccessful, and he showed some fatigue when the final bell sounded, draping himself over the top rope of his corner. The announcer finally called us both in for the decision. Randy assured me as he milled around in the corner with my team that I had done enough to win the bout. The red corner was full, as my wife, brother, and several close friends were there for support. The announcer began the announcement: "And the new United States Heavyweight Champion is—" he paused for effect "— Kevin 'Hurricane' Hudson!" The crowd roared and I had my new belt strapped around me. As I looked up I mouthed the words, "This is for you, Eddie. This is for you."

The victory dinner was sweet that night. My wife was by my side, and my family were there too, along with several of my close friends. Randy and Dale headed back home after the bout concluded. Their six-hour drive wasn't too exciting, but they knew they needed to get back in order for Randy to work the next day. I knew I'd pulled out a great fight that night. I was proud that I'd won the fight even though I wasn't feeling my best. At the victory dinner, the muscular challenger who had barreled down on me for ten rounds walked in. He had a good bit of swelling around his face, and looked like he'd ridden his motorcycle through a hailstorm without a helmet. When I saw this, the pain in my hands began to decrease. The rest of the evening with my hands in ice buckets in the hotel room was a small price to pay for the hitting the mark that night.

"**1** There is a time for everything, and a season for every activity under heaven: **2** a time to be born and a time to die, a time to plant and a time to uproot, **3** a time to kill and a time to heal, a time to tear down and a time to build, **4** a time to weep and a time to laugh, a time to mourn and a time to dance, **5** a time to scatter stones and a time to gather them, a time to embrace and a time to refrain, **6** a time to search and a time to give up, a time to keep and a time to throw away, **7** a time to tear and a time to mend, a time to be silent and a time to speak, **8** a time to love and a time to hate, a time for war and a time for peace." (Ecclesiastes 3:1–8)

SUREFIRE STRATEGY 38: Don't have a plan B. Many times people think to themselves when they begin a new endeavor: "Well, if it doesn't work, I can just get out." That's no way to go at a worthy goal. Many times this type of attitude is the root of failure. It's spilling over into our society in epidemic proportions. Look at the divorce rate. People go into a marriage with this kind of plan B attitude, which undermines the level of commitment each participant has. When I stepped into the ring to fight, whether in a competition or in the gym, there was no plan B. I was planning on winning and going the distance. I didn't win them all, but not because I didn't give it my absolute best. Stepping into the ring each time, I was prepared to be hauled out on a stretcher if necessary. That's the person who wins: the person who believes in his cause so much that even death is okay. As a parent we all know we'd protect our kids with that kind of ferociousness. Let's get ferocious about our success and our ability to perform.

SUREFIRE STRATEGY 39: Wherever you are, *be there*! Life is short, so cherish the time you have with friends and family in a way that shows the importance you place on that particular relationship. You see people sitting in restaurants who are looking down at their cell phones and not speaking with one another. I've sat down at meetings with people, and the first thing they do is pull out their cell phone and set it on the table. That automatically tells me that what we are discussing isn't important, and if that cell phone rang they'd choose that over our in-person conversation. Be respectful of time. It's the one resource you can't manufacture, and there's only a finite amount of it given to any of us.

SUREFIRE STRATEGY 40: Get a pet. Regardless of how bad a day you think you've had, when you come home to a loving pet, it's hard not to cheer up. People with pets live longer, are more productive, and have fewer health issues. Pets are even better than kids sometimes. They don't talk back!

SUREFIRE STRATEGY 41: Move to the side. Moving straight back is dangerous. Life comes at you hard, and if you move in one direction you eventually run out of ring. Learn to move laterally, be flexible, and don't be so set on one solution that you aren't pliable. In the US title match as well as in life, being able to move sideways while I caught my breath and regrouped was the key to victory. It can be the key to survival.

CHAPTER 14

FINAL ROUND

In 2005, I got a call from the president of one of the world's leading kickboxing sanctioning bodies at the time. Chuck Norris was putting together a new concept and needed fighters who really knew their stuff. The president of Chuck's new organization gave me and my brother Shannon "the Cannon" an invitation to compete in the inaugural World Combat League event in Dallas, Texas.

My brother and I both were known for not turning down a good match, and this was something different and maybe the one thing kickboxing needed. I thought this could be the big break. With a guy like Chuck behind the scenes it was sure to be a huge success, and both brothers were in on the ground floor.

We boarded a plane out of our hometown the week of the event. We were both pretty excited about this opportunity, and the fact that we'd would get to hang out with Chuck Norris some. The combat league was team fighting. Each team had five guys and one girl. Each member of the team had to fight one round in the first half of the event and one round in the second half of the event. They'd all fight one three-minute round in a bowl-shaped ring designed for the league. It took some getting used to. The fights were kickboxing, with leg kicks and free-handed knees. You couldn't hold and knee, but you could get inside and throw a knee technique without holding your opponent. My brother and I had both trained hard to be prepared for this fast-paced match and were ready and poised as we headed to Dallas.

The weigh-ins for this event were held in two places. Two teams were weighing at one of Chuck's offices in downtown Dallas. It was a huge building in the center of the city. The other two teams were weighing at the Texas State Fair, which was a big deal with a lot of media coverage. My team were weighing at the office, while the Cannon's team were doing the State Fair weigh-ins. The weigh-ins went well. I made the cut-off weight with no problem. Not eating for a day or so and drinking sparsely was nothing new for me. Once the teams finished weighing, it was off to the local buffet and a good night's rest before the event.

Saturday came and the teams were loaded onto buses and vans to get to the arena by three o'clock in order to prepare and do the normal check-ins with the doctors and do the prefight media coverage. The event was unique in many ways. Teams would pair off against each other. The combatants would fight in a bowl like octagon with no ropes and raised edges. Teams would be called out before the evening started to do a friendly stare-down in the round ring. This was a perfect time for the announcer to work the crowd up and get them excited about the upcoming bouts.

The setup was a little unusual, as each team had a coach who cornered every fighter. The coach hadn't met some of the fighters and was unfamiliar with their fighting styles. My brother and I were on different teams, so we were in different dressing rooms. My team was scheduled to fight first. The Cannon would be watching me compete on a monitor that was set up in his dressing room.

I went through my warm-up routine as best I could with the guys in the room that were on my team. I had gotten one of the coaches to wrap my hands for me. Each member of the team had to be ready to get in the spotlight when the announcer called out his name. I heard my name being called for the next fight. I hurried to get the gloves from the athletic commission official and had a coach put them on. Going to the ring for the world combat league was a solo event. No corner men went with you, and no other person was allowed in the spotlight. I stepped into the light and the crowd roared. Maybe not for me, but for the team—I wasn't sure how many fans I had in Dallas. I trotted down the steps to the yellow line on the floor, which we were supposed to follow to the ring in the center of the arena. The ring for the league had no ropes, and a single step up would put you on the side of it. The ring was curved upward at the edges, so being in the middle of the ring gave you about eighteen flat feet to work with. Chuck's thought here was to keep the fighters in the center of the ring more, and thus keep the action moving. The referees of the Combat League would urge the fighters to fight whenever action lulled the least bit.

I stepped into the center and faced my opponent. My opponent was close to my size, from the Chicago area, with a muscular build and a vast amount of martial arts experience. The referee called us both to attention and gave a brief overview of the Combat League rules: you could sweep, you could knee with no clinch, and you could kick the legs, no elbows. We both acknowledged understanding the rules. The referee, Cecil Peoples—a famous referee in the boxing world—ordered us to back up and get ready for the bell. My opponent and I both stepped back and readied ourselves for the signal to fight. The bell rang out through the arena and the crowd cheered. My opponent and I began to move forward toward the center of the ring. Peoples watched closely as we drew near to one another. I had prepared for a fast-paced fight and, with the hype of the crowd and the referee urging us to engage, I stepped in with a rear leg round kick. But on that day I would make an elementary error that would make me rethink my future fighting opportunities.

I dropped my rear hand just a hair too low as I chambered the kick for delivery. My opponent, slightly quicker on the draw, launched a straight right hand directly at my chin. Making contact when I was on one foot made it even more mind-numbing. When the blow struck, I heard the crowd roar for a second, and then I hit the floor. Lying on the mat in a puddle, I tried to gather myself in the ten-second time limit. I had evidently fallen forward some, then back, pinning one leg behind me. The other leg was straight in front. I was able to gather myself and rise by about the time the referee counted eight. The referee looked into my eyes and said loudly, "Walk forward!" As he stepped forward a pain shot through my right knee, the one that had been bent awkwardly in the fall. Walking forward toward the referee, I also noticed that I had lost my vision on the side the blow had struck. But I couldn't stop the fight, not like this. So I stepped forward anyway and readied myself for the onslaught. Sure enough, when Cecil Peoples said "Fight!" my opponent rushed in for the kill. I began pulling on every bit of energy and will I had to avoid this suddenly overconfident combatant. Despite being half blind and pretty much one-legged, I was able to survive the next half of the round and make it through to the end. Of course, winning that round was impossible after the knockdown and the retreating method of survival I had employed after the knockdown.

At the completion of the round I walked back to the dressing room, following the yellow line laid out on the floor for fighters to exit the arena. This line was so bright a yellow that even a fighter with half a brain could follow it. I managed to make it back to his team's dressing room without letting on that my knee was injured or that my vision was impaired. At this point, the way I saw it, I had about one hour to get my act back together in order to compete in my second round. I sat down on a bench in the dressing room to assess my condition. My quick recovery in the ring had given no indication that the doctors should follow me back. As I sat on the bench, my vision began to un-blur some, but my knee began to swell. I realized that for the first time in my fighting career I was hurt during the match and didn't move forward in retaliation. My mind raced back to my wife at home, my daughter, and my newborn son. I thought to myself, if the vision doesn't come back in this eye, I wouldn't be able to see my son or daughter out of that eye. I thought, is this worth it? Maybe with a family, business, and the lack of time to dedicate to training it could be time to hang up the gloves and not compete anymore.

The coach finally ran through the door between bouts and yelled, "Hurricane, you good?"

"Yes sir," I shouted as I bent my legs and rose from the bench. I got myself standing straight and went to the ice machine down the hall. I had brought an ice bag with me, which is normal equipment for this type of event. I took it down the hall and filled it at the machine and headed back to the locker room. My vision began to clear up further as I sat down again in the same spot. I stretched out my knee and laid the ice bag on it for the next fifteen minutes or so. My teammates all finished their first round and the other two teams began their competition. The Cannon's team was up, and my teammates and I piled around the monitor to watch it. I got a spot in the corner where I could ice the knee and see the monitor. The Cannon did well in his bout, and would actually go on to fight in most of the World Combat League events. He was a talented young fighter and eight years younger than me, so he was ripe for the competition and needed by the League, which was trying to make its way out of obscurity.

I managed to get my knee loosened up for the next round. I stayed standing for the remainder of the halftime show, as they called it. My knee was stiff but able to hold me, and I hoped I'd make it through this next round. I had a plan, which was to try my best to knock this guy out before the end of the round. It wasn't going to be pretty and it probably wasn't going to be with a head kick, but because of my situation at this point, my only chance of winning this round was a knockout.

I began readying myself for the next outing and gloved up with the help of a teammate. I warmed up as best I could without showing any signs of ill health. I made sure that word wouldn't get back to the opposing team that there might be a weak spot in the team. The announcer roused up the crowd again and I made the ascent onto the stage where the spotlight would shine. The announcer called my name and I began the descent to the yellow line. I followed the yellow line into the bowl-shaped ring, making sure not to wobble or limp. The doctors watching the action were keenly aware of each fighter's injuries and shortcomings; however, I was able to slip my bum knee by without detection. I stepped over the lip of the bowl and raised my hands to the crowd, and they cheered. I then was motioned by the referee to come to the center and hear the rules.

As he completed his monologue, my opponent and I stared intently at one another, each trying to instill fear in his opponent. At this level of competition fear was not a factor for either of us. We bumped gloves on the referee's command and backed up, allowing the referee to get between us. The referee looked at my opponent and then at me, making sure we were in position, and then said, *"Fight!"* as he dropped his hand like a sword cutting a watermelon.

We both advanced forward, with my opponent making the first move. The entire three-minute round was competitive, but lackluster in terms of domination. I did enough to keep from falling down or getting pounded, and my opponent attempted to bypass my defensive skills, though with marginal success. The referee urged us both on as the round came to a close. We both ended up in a slugfest in the center of the circle, with the crowd making lots of noise. The bell finally rang and we both shot our gloves toward the sky in celebration of a tough-fought round. The judge's decision came relatively quickly as the referee gathered us in the center of the circle. All three judges scored the bout the same…and the decision did not go my way this time; however, I was glad I hadn't let the team down. Though I was injured, I had finished the fight.

After the referee let go of our hands and directed us to the dressing room, I carefully stepped toward the edge of the circle where it dropped to the arena floor. I stepped off the edge good leg first, in order to hide my bum leg. I made it back to the dressing room and found a spot to sit for a moment. Once I settled down and removed my gear, my next mission was to find the ice bucket again.

I sat in the dressing room for the next twenty minutes or so, icing the knee in order to keep the swelling down. From where I sat I could see the monitor and was able to see my brother win his second bout against a tough opponent. After the ice bag had melted to water I pushed myself up and threw the bag away. I then proceeded to finish removing my wraps and other equipment to prepare to head back to the hotel. My brother finished in his dressing room and we met out in the back of the arena where the vans Norris had arranged to pick up the teams were coming. The ride back to the hotel took about forty minutes, and a good night's rest was in order after a shower and another round of icing the knee. I didn't look forward to the long plane ride the next day, cramped in a coach seat with a swollen stiff knee.

SUREFIRE STRATEGY 42: Don't let your team down. No matter what your profession or passion you'll have to work with a team. As the old adage goes, there is no 'I' in team. In American culture it seems we value the title of "self-made man" or "self-made woman." But there is no such thing as "self-made." The successful person had someone influencing them to achieve their success. This influence could be positive, or it could be negative. A person may have a great relationship with a parent, and the parent may be an inspiration for this person to push through and be successful. A person may have a horrible relationship or no relationship with a parent, and that parent may be the driving force behind this person's success. Either way, there's someone working with you or on you to drive you forward. When you reach a certain level of success in life there will inevitably be a team around you to help you with daily activities. As a team member, you must carry your end of the load to keep the team moving in the proper direction.

SUREFIRE STRATEGY 43: Get a massage once in a while. In our bodies, as humans, we are victims of tension. This tension inhibits proper energy flow and circulation. Much of this tension can be alleviated by stretching and meditation, but a licensed therapeutic deep-tissue massage can clean out those meridians and help get you get back to championship form. Taking time out for self is important, and firing on all cylinders is important. Working out the kinks in our structure through available means is a worthy endeavor.

SUREFIRE STRATEGY 44: Play an instrument. It doesn't matter which instrument you choose; there's just something spectacular about being able to play music. Whether you strum a few chords on the guitar or play a note or two on the piano, playing music soothes the soul. God loves a joyful noise-maybe that's why it's satisfying to make music. It's a wonderful stress reliever to be able to hear a melody you play. Pick up an instrument and take a few lessons, and you'll be surprised by how quickly you start sounding good.

CHAPTER 15

STILL KICKING: THOUGHTS FROM THE HURRICANE

After reading about the rumbles I've had in the ring, you may wonder how I can still think. Well, fortunately God blessed me with a head like a trailer hitch, a chin like a yak, and the fortitude of a wolverine. So the rounds in competition weighed on me some, but not enough to discombobulate my mind. A man told me once that being a champion is not a onetime decision, it's a daily decision. Being a champion and hitting your mark, is about making that decision again and again. Every day the discipline it takes to be a champion and to hit that mark must consciously be made. No one accidently becomes a champion. It takes consistent effort on a daily basis. It's about daily disciplines. Doing the small things daily that accumulate over time. Many times when I was training for a bout, one of my trainers would scream, "I bet your opponent has already finished his training today!" That would fire me up. To think that cat even thought he could beat me and had the gumption to get off the couch and maybe train harder than I did was appalling to me.

My mentor Joe Lewis told his students many times, "Never let an opponent have an advantage over you in physical fitness." That meant you had to outwork him in the gym before the match. To hit that mark, you got to out-work your opponent. That opponent could be fear, lack of family support, lack of funds, or even lack of discipline. You must recognize that opponent and get to work remedying it.

Did I ever fight unprepared? I lost some matches, and those matches were either fought unprepared mentally or physically. I regret those times. But you learn a lot about yourself when you're out of gas and have six or eight rounds to go, with a disciplined fighter in front of you trying to knock your block off. I learned about perseverance. I learned about the power of the mind and heart. There's something to be said when a person overpowers the body's will to quit with the mind's desire not to give up. I set out to accomplish a goal and did it. Did it all turn out the way I had dreamed as a kid, did I hit the mark I intended to as a young fighter? No. But did the process teach me to rely on God, be flexible, and know I can accomplish much if I set my mind to it? Yes.

Finding a passion as a young child with proper guidance allowed me to filter my decisions and choices through a window that few kids—or adults, for that matter—have today. I have great parents, who fostered my passion and drove me to class day after day. This dedication developed a good work ethic in me. Praising a kid for being smart may foster one thing, but praising a kid for hard work fosters another. Praising a kid for hard work develops ambition in that kid. I was fortunate to have people acknowledge my hard work, as well as dedication early on, which led to goal setting, which led to dream development...and those dreams came to fruition.

Working to develop my skills as a martial artist made me who I am today. It taught me so many valuable lessons and led to me being able to work as a professional martial arts teacher for most of my life, instilling the things I learned as a child in adults and kids today.

I remember taking my future wife home to my parents when she and I first met. I introduced her to my mom and dad. They were thrilled to meet this girl I'd spoken so much about. The next day after that meeting I went by my dad's business to see what he thought of her. He told me how nice and pretty she was, and left me with one piece of advice: "Kevin, just don't karate her to death." He didn't mean beat up on her or anything; he meant talk her to death about karate, kickboxing, and my aspirations.

I either heeded his advice or she built up a tolerance to my talking about my passion. She and I have been married for twenty years now, and God has blessed us with three beautiful children. I own two martial arts centers and every day get to influence the community I live in with my teachings. That being said, with influence comes responsibility. I deem it an honor to do what I do, and I take it seriously. I realize that my influence over these people doesn't stop with martial arts; it carries over into character and who I am. I've been blessed to live near a fantastic church that I've become involved with. My family and I see it as our responsibility to be there when we can and serve in the capacity in which God has enabled us. We are all given spiritual gifts and talents. To not use them is an abomination of our character, since we were made in God's image.

I've realized that the process is more important than the destination. Reaching a certain goal or certain level of success is fabulous, but who you become in the process is much more important. The things we achieve are in direct correlation with our character and the investment we place in things we value. Being the best at something is mighty cool, but placing higher value on *being* there than *getting* there is a mistake. It's who we become not what we are that makes the difference.

There are other points that need to be considered in order to get the most out of life. I'd like to share those with you now. This list is not in any order of importance—I'm sure you've realized that. All of these rules are equally important, and any one of them can make a huge difference in your quality of life.

SUREFIRE STRATEGY 45: Learn to sell. Everyone is in sales, whether they realize it or not. You're selling yourself every day. You're selling your opinions. You're selling your personality. Everyone needs to find a service or a product they're passionate about, and proceed to sell it to others. A good salesperson will be able to take a prospect through an orchestrated series of events that culminates in a financial transaction. This teaches you so much about human character, body language, and communication. In life, the only time you get paid financially is when you ask a person to pay you. It could be in an interview for a job or a door-to-door sales presentation. Learning to sell teaches you how to better sell yourself.

SUREFIRE STRATEGY 46: Visit an orphanage. In my travels, I've been privileged to visit orphanages. Seeing children in an environment that lack a stable, traditional family is a humbling experience. Toddlers walk up to you just to be held. One orphanage in a country where they do not allow international adoption and that runs exclusively on donations from individuals really struck a chord with me. The orphanage had kids who were fourteen and fifteen, and had been dropped off on the doorstep as infants. I try to support this type of ministry in any way I can. In James 1:27, James commands us to help the orphans and widows. Were it not for the grace of God it could have been me. In addition to visiting an orphanage, to gain perspective you also need to visit a third-world country. Go visit a place where they don't have many paved roads and the average wage earner earns $10 or less per day and see how they live. This could be done on a mission trip or just on your own.

SUREFIRE STRATEGY 47: Watch the Andy Griffith Show. I know you're thinking, "That crazy Southern boy thinks I need to watch an antiquated television show about a hick town in North Carolina?" But this show, in my opinion, is some of the best family-oriented entertainment ever filmed. Each show has a theme. The topics include friendship, handling controversy, dealing with bullies, parenting, and many more. For one of my birthdays, my family purchased me the entire eight seasons on DVD. I sit down with one or more of my children once in a while and watch one. They make great conversational and teaching moments for a parent and a child.

There you have it: forty-seven surefire steps to put into place in order to get the most out of this world. These forty-seven steps are sure to put some pep in your step and a smile on your face. Don't feel overwhelmed; just remember that implementing one of these steps makes a difference—a good difference. The more you can act on them, the better life will become-Lord willing. It all starts with you.

The strongest muscle in your body is between your ears, and that's the one that needs the training. Work it just like you'd work any muscle. Keep it active and limber. If you use your mind and have a good connection with your Creator, there's no telling how far you can go. We were made in God's image and sometimes we, as humans, discount our ability to do miraculous things. Jesus was a miracle worker. The world was created out of nothing, so dreaming big dreams and creating the life you design in your dreams is God-like. He created something from nothing and he gave us the ability to do the same in a certain sense. When I started training as a kid, I dreamed of being a champion. I wasn't one at that time, and many people who trained with me or came into contact with me discouraged me from pursuing that dream. They would say things like, "You'll never make it," or "Don't waste your time." Those comments didn't distract me one bit. I kept pushing and kept training as a champion would, because I knew I could do it.

You can do much if you set your mind to work hard, stay focused, and disciplined. I know you've heard that before, but it's true. Is it always going to be easy? Is it always going to work out exactly like you thought it would? Maybe not, but at least you can say you stayed the course. Remember, the process is more important than the destination. It's not what you become in the end; it's the process that's important, and how that process changes you. Hopefully these 47 Surefire Strategies have got you thinking and hopefully you'll use them to *Hit the Mark* your Creator designed for you.

Keep kicking, and God bless!

APPENDIX

SUREFIRE STRATEGY 1: Find your passion

SUREFIRE STRATEGY 2: Love your mom.

SUREFIRE STRATEGY 3: Take action.

SUREFIRE STRATEGY 4: Stay humble.

SUREFIRE STRATEGY 5: Learn to take a punch.

SUREFIRE STRATEGY 6: Exercise and eat right.

SUREFIRE STRATEGY 7: Stay in school or, if you're out, continue to pursue your education on your own.

SUREFIRE STRATEGY 8: Give thanks. Be grateful.

SUREFIRE STRATEGY 9: Remember you are who you associate with.

SUREFIRE STRATEGY 10: Be by yourself. Learn to be alone.

SUREFIRE STRATEGY 11: Cry sometimes.

SUREFIRE STRATEGY 12: Fail forward.

SUREFIRE STRATEGY 13: Trust people.

SUREFIRE STRATEGY 14: Be faithful and true.

SUREFIRE STRATEGY 15: Keep your promises.

SUREFIRE STRATEGY 16: Keep a journal.

SUREFIRE STRATEGY 17: Become a constant reader.

SUREFIRE STRATEGY 18: Be careful not to believe everything you hear.

SUREFIRE STRATEGY 19: Prosper where you're planted.

SUREFIRE STRATEGY 20: Run your own business.

SUREFIRE STRATEGY 21: Write a budget and try to stick with it.

SUREFIRE STRATEGY 22: Spend time talking with the elderly.

SUREFIRE STRATEGY 23: Study history.

SUREFIRE STRATEGY 24: Stay pure.

SUREFIRE STRATEGY 25: Be careful not to jump on bandwagons.

SUREFIRE STRATEGY 26: Give. In the Bible it says you need to give your time, talents, and finances.

SUREFIRE STRATEGY 27: Read the Bible.

SUREFIRE STRATEGY 28: Go to church.

SUREFIRE STRATEGY 29: Don't do drugs.

SUREFIRE STRATEGY 30: Get really good at one thing.

SUREFIRE STRATEGY 31: Teach something.

SUREFIRE STRATEGY 32: Have good posture.

SUREFIRE STRATEGY 33: Be slow to sign your name to official documents.

SUREFIRE STRATEGY 34: Look people in the eye.

SUREFIRE STRATEGY 35: Say "yes ma'am" and "no ma'am," "yes sir" and "no sir."

SUREFIRE STRATEGY 36: Don't use up all of your best resources in the first round.

SUREFIRE STRATEGY 37: Enjoy the journey.

SUREFIRE STRATEGY 38: Don't have a plan B.

SUREFIRE STRATEGY 39: Wherever you are, *be there*!

SUREFIRE STRATEGY 40: Get a pet.

SUREFIRE STRATEGY 41: Move to the side.

SUREFIRE STRATEGY 42: Don't let your team down

SUREFIRE STRATEGY 43: Get a massage once in a while.

SUREFIRE STRATEGY 44: Play an instrument.

SUREFIRE STRATEGY 45: Learn to sell.

SUREFIRE STRATEGY 46: Visit an orphanage.

SUREFIRE STRATEGY 47: Watch the Andy Griffith Show.

Printed in the United States
By Bookmasters